Snowball's Chance

David Lynch

London • New York • Cleveland • New Orleans
Keene, New Hampshire

Faulkner Press
New York, New York

Faulkner Press and colophon are registered trademarks
of Faulkner Publishing, LLC.

For information about bulk purchase discounts, subsidiary rights, and
author appearances, please contact Faulkner Publishing, LLC
by email: publisher@thefaulknerpress.com
or visit our website: www.thefaulknerpress.com

Library of Congress Cataloging-in-Publication Data is available.

Manufactured in the United States.

10 9 8 7 6 5 4 3 2

Interior design and production: Joy Cimino and Nate Faulkner

Cover design by Courtney Jane DiJulius and Michael McGrath, Jr.

Photo credits listed.

ISBN 13: 978-0-9977700-1-8

Contents

To Nancy, Scott, Bridget, and Colleen

I love you more than horseradish.

CHAPTER ONE

The Warning

IT WAS MID-NOVEMBER 1985 and I was feeling pretty proud of myself.

"Look kid. You got lucky this one time." Frank Chukayne (pronounced "Shu-kay-nee") looked across his desk at me.

I felt like a fifth-grader sent to see the principal. But Chukayne was no school principal. He was intimidating, unlit cigar sticking out of his mouth to the side, halfway between his front teeth and the left molars.

It was a scene out of an old mobster movie from the 40's. Chukayne was like Edward G. Robinson.

"Now listen here kid," he continued. "I said listen up. Pay attention. Then maybe you won't get hurt. You payin' attention kid?"

I had been summoned to the office of Chukayne, the consigliere to Mayor Anthony J. Giunta also known as "Fat Tony".

Frank Chukayne, at age 63, was part of that mysterious inner circle of the Coalition Party. His official title listed on the reader board when you entered City Hall was Executive Director. Nobody knew what that meant as the position didn't exist in the city charter or book of ordinances.

But it didn't take long for me to figure out that he was the man Fat Tony used to make sure the staff at City Hall toed the line when it came to Coalition politics.

A story making the rounds at the time involved an employee in the city's wastewater treatment plant who loved his job. Frank Chukayne came to visit his home one balmy Saturday afternoon. The city worker was washing his brand new red Chevy convertible when Chukayne appeared with a big smile and a can of Turtle Wax. They made small talk but the employee was baffled as to the motive behind the Executive Director's appearance.

Chukayne was just getting back into his shiny black Fleetwood Cadillac when he asked about the car payment for the Chevrolet. He told the fellow that it would sure be hard to make that payment without a good income such as that provided by the City of Euclid. The not so subtle message was clear: this young man had not purchased tickets to Coalition events and it did not go unnoticed. He never missed a single Coalition potluck dinner or raffle after that. And he never missed making a car payment.

Chukayne had silver hair slicked back with a neat part on the right side. His slate blue eyes stared out at you from behind high fashion ebony frame eyeglasses. He dressed impeccably in Armani suits with a beautiful silk pocket square, his right pinky adorned with a big diamond ring.

He carried himself with a certain elegance that belied his role as manager of political executions for the Coalition empire. The Coalition reigned supreme. They were the power in the city. You weren't supposed to challenge them.

But I had picked off one of their lieutenants. George Carson was their guy, the Ward Three Councilman. In a surprise, like a hidden sniper, I had defeated George Carson just a few days before to become the new Ward Three Councilman.

At age 28.

That's why I had been asked to appear at City Hall. Chukayne was willing to tip his hat to my chutzpah. But he wanted me to know my place.

I wasn't really a threat. Even with my victory, the Mayor and the Coalition party had an automatic six out of nine votes on city council whenever they wanted. Six votes still meant passage of anything Fat Tony and the Coalition desired.

After all, I was just a kid. But Frank Chukayne wanted me to know that I'd be allowed to survive if I stuck to my minor role in the dramatic enterprises of the Independent Coalition Party.

It was his job to slap down uprisings from upstarts.

"Take care of your constituents and stay out of our way," he said. "We'll send the service department out to respond to citizen complaints when you pass them on to us. You'll be a popular young councilman and the Coalition will leave you alone."

"Follow my advice and you'll be just fine. Stay in your place and don't get too big for your britches."

He didn't tell me what would happen if I didn't follow his advice.

He didn't tell me what would happen if I used the council floor to criticize Fat Tony and the overspending good old boy system at City Hall. But I figured ignoring advice from Chukayne was not going to lead to a successful career.

He smiled a little.

Creepy.

Frightening.

I sat there and listened. I wasn't playing it cool. It's just that I was a little terrified. Silence was better than stuttering out some halting acknowledgment that I was a lamb among wolves.

Very hungry wolves. The euphoria I experienced on election night just a few days earlier was just a memory.

These guys were serious.

Frank Chukayne was a dapper enforcer of employee allegiance: elegant and evil.

I wanted to leave this room filled with the air of monolithic control. I half expected to hear Frank whisper Don Corleone's "Nobody goes against the family".

Finally, it was over and I got up to leave.

"One more thing," Frank added. "Remember this. Nobody runs against Tony. Don't ever get such a thought in your head." He repeated it slowly just in case I didn't fully understand the message. "Nobody runs against Tony."

This story is filled with larger-than-life characters. Chukayne is just the first of many that I'll introduce you to as I tell you what happened in 1987.

All these people are real and everything you read here is exactly as it happened. Go ahead and doubt me, but I'm telling you it all took place as I describe in this book. It's an epic tale filled with outsized personalities, heroes and cowards.

I quietly slipped out of City Hall to the parking lot. I swear I heard the strains of the Godfather theme playing in the background. As I headed for home I couldn't get one thought out of my mind.

Maybe I should run against Tony.

CHAPTER TWO

The Coalition

THREE MILLION ACRES along the southern shore of Lake Erie constituted what became known as the Connecticut Western Reserve in 1795 as a result of some questionable treaties with Indian tribes. Then in 1796 the entire parcel was sold by the Connecticut state legislature to a corporation called the Connecticut Land Company.

One of the corporate officers, Moses Cleaveland, was a brigadier general in the Connecticut militia, having served with George Washington in the Continental Army. He and his fellow shareholders envisioned the Western Reserve as the key to tremendous wealth in the newly founded United States.

In 1803, Cleaveland was commissioned to lead an expedition to properly stake the corporation's land claim, establishing boundaries and installing permanent markers.

Just under seventy brave souls made the dangerous trip into what would eventually become Northeast Ohio, many of them surveyors and former military. In this mostly unexplored land, maps of any detail were virtually nonexistent, making surveyors indispensable.

Forty-one members of the expedition became disgruntled and asked for the opportunity to establish their own settlement. The general agreed. The splinter group named the township after Euclid, the father of modern geometry whose principles lay at the heart of the surveying profession. Moses Cleaveland carried on westward with the remaining members of his team, establishing what would eventually become the City of Cleveland at the mouth of the mighty Cuyahoga

River. The City's name was a tribute to the general who bravely guided that original stalwart band, the first "A" in Cleaveland dropped because a newspaper typesetter needed to eliminate one letter from a headline.

Because the Cuyahoga emptied into the Great Lake Erie, Cleveland grew into a major port of commerce in the young nation. Euclid puttered along as a lazy little village to the east of the big city, known mostly as a place of vineyards and dirt roads.

By the early 1900s, Cleveland had become a major metropolis, replete with steel plants, factories, and breweries. Immigrants poured into Cleveland looking for jobs and the American dream. The 1910 national census lists Cleveland as the 5th largest municipality in the country.

Euclid grew more slowly than her gigantic neighbor city on its western border, lacking the roads, sewers, waterlines, and other infrastructure needed to promote development.

Times were tough for the municipality as the depression took its toll. The city government, unable to pay its own employees, printed its own City of Euclid dollar bills in 1934 to compensate municipal workers. They could be spent only at stores within Euclid proper, the local government promising to give authentic United States currency to the retailers at a future date.

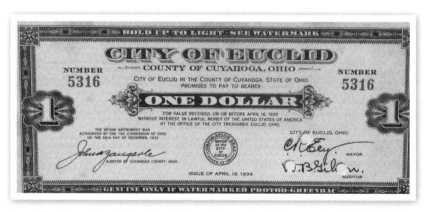

One official City of Euclid Dollar Bill issued in 1934, valid in only one city in the U.S.A.

But in 1935 things began to happen. Euclid City officials permitted the placement of slot machines all over town in return for a cut of the action. Of course, gambling was illegal but Euclid needed the commerce. The taverns saw the slots as an extra profit center that other Ohio cities wouldn't tolerate. The slots led to numbers rackets and before you knew it, Euclid was a pretty wild town. Vice flourished because the local constable was well compensated to look the other way.

Boozing and gambling made Euclid a pretty wild town.

Although City Hall finally had money, boozing and gambling had turned Euclid into a mecca for good times and graft.

Ken Sims, a young lawyer in town, had just about all he could stomach of the crooked city leaders. He was sick of what Euclid had been allowed to become and sick of the way the mayor and other officials lined their pockets with bribes from saloon operators and bookies.

So he launched a new idea.

He publicly challenged Republicans and Democrats to come together to form a new organization, The Euclid Independent Coalition Party, designed to run the rats out of town.

The entrenched city officials, led by Mayor Charles Ely, weren't above using violence and intimidation to squash the Sims rebellion. However, Sims had gotten the attention of the press, and editorials fanned the flames of insurrection against the corrupt Ely administration.

Ely, already Mayor for twelve years, ran the town with an iron fist. When shots were fired at a reporter who had criticized Ely, the scribe filed a police report. The reporter was immediately jailed.

As election day approached, Coalition supporters were taken to police headquarters for questioning at midnight. The Sims group was gripped by a sense of uncertainty and fear.

Mayor Ely's henchmen were tough and intimidating.

Despite this, Sims was courageous in making impassioned speeches, telling the world that he was going to clean up City Hall with his brave new Coalition concept.

It worked.

Honest law-abiding citizens were inspired by this dynamic youthful barrister and he was swept into office as the new mayor in 1937. Heads rolled. Mayor Ken Sims, with his new Coalition Party, eliminated the gambling and the after-hours joints.

And he cleansed Euclid of the graft. Euclid almost overnight became known as an honest town where new developers could hope to build without the need to pay off politicians.

Ken Sims was the new sheriff in town and he wore a white hat. The Coalition, led by the charismatic Sims, carried on that way for decades. The Coalition became the standard for good honest government welcoming both Democrats and Republicans into the fold.

This union of Democrats and Republicans made Euclid a unique place. The Coalition established a city charter that made each city election non-partisan. The party affiliation of the candidate essentially became irrelevant in the city. Whether Democrat or Republican, by law, you couldn't be identified as either on the ballot.

Euclid did indeed have local Republican and Democratic clubs to deal with state and national party politics, but as you'd expect, they were controlled by the Coalition in each instance. Mayor Sims had been a Republican but The Coalition Party had equal numbers of Democrats and Republicans.

From 1937 forward, the Coalition candidates dominated local elections in Euclid. For a long time, every member of the Council was Coalition.

World War II marked the beginning of tremendous industrial growth in Euclid. Factories for General Motors, Euclid Road Machinery, Chase Brass, Addressograph Multigraph, and TRW employed thousands of machinists cranking out the needs of the military industrial complex.

In the 1950's and 1960's, fueled by the post-war baby boom, Euclid became a target location for new young families. Churches and schools sprang up everywhere all over town to keep up with the demand created with the opening of one new housing development after another. Everyone wanted to move into Euclid.

Euclid remained boomtown right into the 1970's and the Coalition, with its legendary Mayor Sims, rode this wave of prosperity.

Ken Sims in his heyday: He was a legend.

As Mayor Sims approached the sunset of his fabulous career in City Hall, people began to notice some cracks in the Coalition concept.

The Coalition had prided itself as nonpartisan, embracing all political parties within its ranks. But what was becoming apparent was the following: if you didn't join the Coalition, the Coalition didn't want to hear what you had to say. Sims was aging and ailing when he finally announced his retirement in June of 1970.

Unfortunately, it was too late. Sims had allowed other Coalitionists, much lesser men than he, to take the reins of the machine he had engineered so many years earlier.

Worse, Coalition leaders had become fat, lazy, and ultimately crooked. The old saying is true: *absolute power corrupts absolutely.* This unraveling of the lofty concepts established by Sims grew worse over time and it carried through to the election of 1987.

One of the characteristics of the post-Sims Coalition was nepotism. The Coalition leaders began hiring their relatives. It was not unusual to have three generations from one Coalition family all working various city jobs at the same time.

Mayor Giunta himself had relatives spread throughout the local government. His son worked in the engineering department, his brother in the parks department, and various in-laws were sprinkled around the city payroll. Even Giunta's father got in on the act, serving as a city surveyor.

The Directors of various departments almost always had family on the city payroll although they tried not to have the relative working directly for their kin. Police Chief Payne was an exception to this rule as his son and his grandson served as police patrolmen.

The real stench began to come from city contracts. Cash went from cement and asphalt contractors into the pockets of city leaders on a regular basis. City contracts were awarded to a select few who shared their wealth with Euclid officials willing to fix the bidding process. A frequent trick was to declare some big project to be an emergency, not subject to bidding.

But perhaps even more disgusting was the blatant racism that fueled Coalition politics.

Euclid was a virtually all-white city of just under 70,000 people in 1967. However, its western border abutted the City of Cleveland's eastern boundary. The demographic shifts of the 1950s and 1960s saw thousands of African-American families push east against the Euclid border.

The Coalition was open about their pledge to stem the tide of racial integration. The Coalition candidates swore they would not permit penetration of that border.

The primary tools used to preserve Euclid's whiteness were the police and the judge. "Driving while black" was an unofficial crime. Sadly, this horrible concept is still applied against minorities in many towns today. But for the Coalition of the 50's, 60's, 70's, and 80's, it was an enforcement tool that worked.

The front page of the *Euclid News Journal* in March of 1952 is instructive in understanding the thinking in City Hall on the subject of race. This edition featured a large picture of five Euclid policemen wearing blackface as they promoted the department's annual Minstrel show. The 1952 show was called "Dis is de life."

This edition of the local paper featured police in blackface in 1952.

For minorities in Euclid, it definitely wasn't "de life".

If you had a police scanner during the 1970's and 1980's in Euclid, you would occasionally hear an officer radio into dispatch that he had encountered an "L-O-C". This stood for a "Load Of Coal", that is, an automobile full of black people. The occupants of said vehicle were fortunate if the law enforcement official merely accompanied them to the city border as opposed to initiating an arrest. Getting the minorities out of the city, though, seemed to satisfy the mighty Coalition's objective of keeping Euclid white.

Despite Jackie Robinson jolting Americans from their passive indifference toward racism as he wore the uniform of the Brooklyn Dodgers in 1947, the Euclid administration was proof that the days of Jim Crow were alive and well in this bustling suburb featuring lush neighborhoods and vibrant industry.

Black families kept on their side of the border. Who wanted to spend the night in jail or worse just because one wandered into Coalition territory?

When Carl Stokes was elected the first black mayor of a major metropolitan city in Cleveland in 1967, many Euclid citizens had this thought: blacks may now have their own mayor in Cleveland, but they don't need to come into our neighborhoods here in peaceful Euclid.

Charismatic Carl Stokes with his son,
Carl Jr. who provided an endorsement for this book.

With Euclid Judge Robert Niccum sticking it to every non-Caucasian, the cops and the judge were a nice little one-two punch in the face of racial justice. Essentially, black people feared the City of Euclid and stayed out. This added to the political power of the Coalition.

Sadly, the Coalition party continued to practice racial politics right up to the time that the 1987 mayoral election came along. Sure, the Coalition of 1987 was powerful, but Mayor Sims' ideal no longer existed. The Euclid Coalition party had degenerated into the embodiment of the evil Ken Sims sought to destroy. The Coalition was corrupt, wasteful, and morally compromised by its hateful racism. But it did have an unequaled track record of political success. Since 1937, not one candidate had defeated the Coalition candidate for Mayor.

Mayor Sims had only one serious opponent during his long tenure in the mayor's seat. In 1959, some Democrats broke away from the Coalition. Ed Eckart, billing himself as a "true Democrat", tried to unseat the legendary Sims. Eckart was easily defeated and Sims' victory evidenced the continuing faith that the people had in the Coalition concept.

Sims retired in 1970 and passed the Coalition mayor's baton to City Council President Harry Knuth. Knuth lacked Sims' charisma and the mayor's seat almost fell into non-Coalition hands in 1971 when Knuth's challenger, 27 year-old councilman Tim McCormack, narrowly missed an upset by 381 votes.

Joe Farrell almost broke the Coalition streak by coming close to beating Mayor Giunta in 1979, but he fell short. By this time, Law Director Pat Rocco had taken the helm of the Coalition and Euclid's most powerful political entity kept rolling into 1987: that's 50 years without losing a Mayor's race.

That's what the Coalition's next Mayoral opponent would be up against. Running for mayor against The Coalition was like being tied to a post until King Kong left his lair in the jungle to find the next human sacrifice offered to appease his wrath and his lust for blood.

Who would be nuts enough to be tied to that post?

CHAPTER THREE

Prelude

EUCLID WAS BOOMING during World War II, factories churning out torpedoes and tanks by the tens of thousands.

Euclid Homes, a 500-unit apartment complex, was constructed just at the outset of the war on 200th Street in western Euclid. It was intended as a temporary project, with factory workers taking up residence there only to return to their place of origin after conclusion of the war.

The single-story apartments were tiny but serviceable for the machinists and their families all focused on providing American troops with the weapons of war.

Fast forward to the 1980s.

Euclid Homes still existed, except it has now been converted to low-income housing, most of it ramshackle and poorly maintained.

And unfortunately, owned by the City of Euclid. People were beginning to notice. The City of Euclid had a problem.

The Coalition brain trust solved the problem by selling the entire complex to a single developer. His name was Paul Voinovich, a powerful political operative whose brother George was a rising political star soon to be elected governor of Ohio. It smacked of another political deal made by Coalition Law Director Pat Rocco in a smoke-filled room.

When I arrived on the scene as the new councilman in 1986, Voinovich had defaulted on his promise to convert the complex into attractive condominiums. Paul Voinovich was collecting rent from poor people living in substandard conditions and the boys of the Coalition were responsible for the whole mess.

Councilman Joe Farrell went ballistic when Voinovich was awarded the property but there was little he could do. He didn't have the votes to stop Rocco from concluding the deal.

And now, with Voinovich doing nothing, things were really beginning to stink.

Voinovich approached the city in the spring of 1986 and asked to change his arrangement to allow for commercial retail development.

George Voinovich, left, was an outstanding leader, honest and dedicated to the people of Ohio. Brother Paul, on the right, not so much.

Instead of keeping his promises, Voinovich made a deal with Rocco for the development of a shopping center and a nursing home.

The Three Musketeers, Councilmen Joe Farrell, Mark Jochum, and David Lynch, voted no when the legislation came up for a roll call. But the rest of City Council, blindly following the City Hall Coalition agenda, rewarded Voinovich for his neglect by approving the new pact.

As usual, the three city council voices in the wilderness were defeated in a vain attempt to slow down the Coalition train that continued roaring down the track.

In September of 1986, there was no sign that Paul Voinovich was even living up to this amended deal. Unbelievable! I was particularly disturbed because Euclid Homes was located in my own Ward 3. The residents there were my constituents. I told the law director to draft legislation requiring monthly written reports from the city building department related to Paul Voinovich's compliance.

Rocco balked, claiming that Voinovich's progress was none of council's business. The administration would keep an eye on things, he said. Council, he opined, did not have the right to require written updates.

I challenged Rocco on the floor of the Council. I accused him of stonewalling the legislation because he wanted to keep the Council in the dark regarding Voinovich's dawdling.

Rocco was enraged. He demanded an apology in a front-page story in the Sun Journal News, the weekly paper that covered City Hall.

It was now my move in this high-stakes chess game.

I sued Rocco. I filed a *Mandamus* action, a special lawsuit against a public official to force performance of a public duty. The court papers argued that Rocco's indifference to my request violated his obligations as law director under the City Charter.

I'll never forget that showdown at the Eighth District Court of Appeals (*Mandamus* can be filed at the appellate level). On one side of a 30-foot conference table in the imposing oak room in the Old County Courthouse sat Rocco, Giunta, and six highly paid lawyers from one of the most powerful law firms in Ohio.

The city's lead attorney was Anthony Garofoli, the former President of the Cleveland City Council with a reputation as a "fixer". Garofoli was also known as the Cleveland Mafia's lawyer. Tangling with Garofoli wasn't what I had in mind when I initiated the litigation against Rocco.

On the other side of the massive table sat...me. All by myself, representing myself.

The appellate magistrate made it clear he felt my position to be well taken. He suggested that Rocco might want to soften his opposition, given the City Charter's clear directive to satisfy a councilman's simple request for draft legislation.

Rocco agreed to prepare the requested legislation. He looked across the table at me with those dark, deep-set eyes, seething.

Case over.

The papers reported it as a victory for this young upstart councilman in Euclid. Rocco pooh-poohed the whole thing, claiming he intended to eventually prepare the legislation all along.

Later that night following Rocco's capitulation, Farrell and Jochum congratulated me as we met at Tradewinds, a popular bar right down the street from Euclid Homes. I had earned my stripes.

Maybe I was a rookie, but I had demonstrated the necessary guts to generate respect from my brethren in this ragtag outnumbered army.

Unfortunately, I had made an enemy of Rocco especially.

Farrell toasted me, raising his glass and bellowing, "Here's to the young buck who stuck his neck out with Rocco holding the ax."

He told me to be careful. He knew Rocco.

And he was right.

CHAPTER FOUR

The Meeting

AS A NON-COALITIONIST, I was now part of the loyal opposition.

On the previous edition of this nine-man City Council, two members were constantly outvoted by the powerful knee-jerk Fat Tony contingent. The two brave souls were Councilman at large Joe Farrell and Ward Two Councilman Mark Jochum.

Their political life consisted of two numbers: seven and two. That was the outcome of every important City Council vote.

7 to 2.

7 to 2.

7 to 2.

Over and over.

Joe Farrell once joked that he was going to print a T-shirt for his Council re-election campaign that just had "7-2" printed on the front and the back. Everyone would know what that meant. It was generally viewed by the Coalition that having a couple of councilmen who disagreed with the administration was a good idea. After all, what would it look like if Fat Tony's agenda was continually rubberstamped nine to nothing.

Farrell and Jochum were allowed to exist because the Coalition wanted the public to think someone was keeping them honest.

That's why this minority of two rarely faced any serious Coalition competition for their own City Council seats. Farrell and Jochum were supposed to spout off so that the rest of City Council could pretend to consider their alternate view. The Coalition needed them.

Occasionally, the gang of seven would caucus and hatch a plan to pass a Farrell or Jochum inspired resolution to encourage the public perception that City Council was a deliberative body, a bastion of thoughtful debate.

It wasn't.

But Farrell and Jochum weren't faking it. They saw what was happening and they fought like hell to at least slow down the machine. They just couldn't get any traction.

So when I came along, the gang of seven became the gang of six and you know what happened.

6-3.

6-3.

6-3.

And so on.

I thought that this must be what a coal miner feels like after his first few days on the job. Is this what it's always going to be like until I either die of black lung or I kill myself?

This two-year term on City Council was going to be rough.

So the three of us pecked away at each meeting, constantly overruled and outvoted.

Occasionally we would land a punch that irritated the Mayor. It didn't accomplish much but it let the administration know that we weren't complete pushovers.

Unfortunately, the three of us were like kindergartners thrown into the ring with Mike Tyson. Our little jabs were hardly noticed.

We were a necessary irritation.

So it was with a sense of fatalistic resignation that the three of us met in January of 1987 to discuss the election coming up later that same year in November. All three of us were certain we could easily win re-election to another two-year term on council. The Coalition was willing to allow us our limited territory.

But what about the Mayor? Fat Tony was up for re-election to his third term. Should one of us challenge him, I asked?

Now understand, I was the new kid on the block. Both Farrell and Jochum had logged years of faithful service battling against the abusive practices of The Coalition.

They had earned the privilege to run for Mayor ahead of me, of course. They had dibs on such a challenge.

But Joe and Mark didn't want to go through that again. Both had run for Mayor previously and lost. Joe had competed for the city's top post twice without success.

Both had been ruthlessly attacked by the Coalition during those mayoral runs.

Farrell and Jochum were good men who loved their families. But both of these fine gentlemen had seen the gears of the machine grind up their idealism and their innocence.

It's not that they were scared. They were scarred.

Farrell and Jochum had families that didn't want to repeat the pain of taking on the Coalition head-on again. The Coalition had painted Farrell and Jochum as radicals trying to bring a dangerous element into Euclid–black people.

And it worked.

Of course, Tony had some help one year. In that election of 1979, both Joe and Mark ran at the same time.

Three mayoral candidates. That made it easy for Tony. It's hard to be the loyal opposition candidate when there are two loyal opposition candidates on the ballot at the same time.

Regardless, the political strategy meeting held in my living room seemed to conclude with the three of us resigned to re-election while Fat Tony and the Coalition coasted along for another four-year term.

My wife Nancy had lived in Euclid since the first grade and she chimed in. She pointed out that the three-candidate mayoral race of 1979 saw Fat Tony elected with just under 50% of the vote in his column. A single candidate might have a shot.

Joe and Mark rolled their eyes. Mark stated the obvious. A single candidate would be out there all by himself.

Alone against the power. Alone against the Coalition. Alone against the machine. We laughed about the absurdity of such an idea.

Joe and Mark went home. Nancy and I sat down to talk.

I was too young.

Too inexperienced.

And too ignorant to know any better.

I was going to run against Fat Tony.

CHAPTER FIVE

Now That's Italian

NANCY AND I had come to a pretty momentous decision and we were nervously excited. Even a pair of novices could see that running for Mayor of Euclid was a pretty big deal. We looked for someone close to us and trustworthy to discuss the proposition. When it came to knowledge of local politics, few could match our neighbor behind us by the name of Art Bolon.

Art Bolon was a retired firefighter for the City of Euclid. His son worked for the fire department as well. At age 71, he was somewhat of a political junkie, keeping his ear to the ground, exchanging gossip and rumors with his friends, other retirees. He had informed me that I had a good chance against George Carson in the Ward Three council race, but he said it would be close. Art was dead on with that prediction.

Art's opinion was also valuable because he was pure Italian, a real *paisan*. He used to go fishing with his friends and then come home to cook up some kind of authentic dish involving fish and pasta. Art even made his own wine at home, often trying to educate me on the finer points of winemaking Italian style. Occasionally Art would revert to some Italian dialect, selecting a word or phrase for which the King's English was inadequate. Art used to explain that his dark complexion was a result of his being from Sicily where a deep tan was the only defense against the relentless sun.

Art was a real *gumba*, definitely old-school. He was friendly with Tony Giunta, both hanging out at the Italian-American club in the neighboring suburb of Wickliffe, Ohio. Art always told me how politically aware the Italians were in Euclid. After the Slovenians, he said, they were even more important as a voting block than the Irish. Being Irish, I used to debate with him on this subject. But then he would point out the domination of Giunta and Rocco and I would concede the point.

Art loved our family. In the few short years that we lived just north of him in 1987, we had grown to love him as well. He loved to pick up our kids and hold them, often tossing them up in the air, only to catch them and give them a big kiss.

He especially loved our little Colleen. Colleen would spend hours in the afternoon sitting on Art's back patio, just watching him engaged in some project, from installing a new fence to cleaning the fish from his latest catch.

As toddlers, Scott and Bridget used to sit on the back stoop of our home, making various drawings, almost always awful, using crayons and construction paper. Art would saunter by and inquire of the kids if the masterpieces were for sale. Of course they were, said Bridget: a nickel a picture. Art, ever the softie, usually paid twenty-five cents each for the stuff.

Between my career as a prosecutor downtown and new member of city council, I was frequently away on weekday nights. I could always count on Art to check in on Nancy and the kids in my absence. We had been adopted by our own little Godfather and it gave us a great sense of security.

Another thing about Art was that he was always bringing us something to eat, usually something he had made himself. One specialty was his concoction of oyster crackers soaked in olive oil, garlic, and ranch dressing. It was a snack from heaven. On the more gourmet end of things was Art's famous linguini with clam sauce. It was beyond anything I had ever had before. The old country came to my house when Art brought these special dishes over for sampling.

*Art Bolan: Now **that's** Italian!*

I can't tell you how many times I borrowed from Art's vast collection of tools, only to have him demonstrate proper usage in a way that basically had Art finishing the project for me. I wasn't very handy around the house and Art was delighted to help.

Nancy and I knew from experience that Art would tell us the truth when it came to anything, especially politics. Since he was so accurate about my city council race, we thought it not a bad idea to see what Art's thinking was regarding my run for mayor.

At first he laughed out loud. Then he became serious and rubbed his chin and lower lip as he often did when in a pensive mood.

Silence.

He looked at me with those penetrating eyes of his. The Sicilian proclaimed, "You don't have a snowball's chance in hell of beating Mayor Giunta." We told him that we appreciated his honesty.

And then we went home, swallowed hard, and tried to figure out how to overcome the odds. Art Bolon was rarely wrong in such matters. Despite that, we knew he'd be pulling for us. How could we find the secret to overcoming the challenge that lay before us?

We had no idea.

CHAPTER SIX

Fat Tony

THE MAYOR, at age 59 in 1987, was arguably the most powerful politician in Northeast Ohio.

In addition to his lofty post at City Hall, Tony Giunta sat on the board of the Regional Transit Authority (RTA), the behemoth that controlled all the buses and rapid-transit rail transportation for commuters throughout Cuyahoga County. It was one of the biggest systems in the world, and Mayor Tony was the key man. The Regional Transit Authority had recently acquired Euclid's own municipal bus system and as a result had become a national player in the transit system business.

Some groused that the Coalition had sold out, giving up the city's efficient, well-run bus system in exchange for the powerful post on the RTA board. Regardless, Mayor Giunta's board seat on the RTA gave him political power and patronage opportunities that went well beyond the borders of the City of Euclid. Tony was powerful as mayor, but now he was also rubbing elbows with senators, congressmen, and members of the President's cabinet.

The story of Tony's rise to become mayor is a tale of a man who found himself in the right place at the right time.

Law Director Pat Rocco's pick of Anthony Giunta to head the Coalition political machine made some scratch their heads when Mayor Sustarsic was forced out. After all, Giunta had made his reputation as an expert in basic city services such as snow removal and trash collection. He was not known as a keen political operator. But Rocco had found a man of the people. Fat Tony was first elected mayor in 1979. He was loved by the community because he was the anti-politician.

At 5 foot 7 1/2 inches tall, Tony was not flashy. He was clearly overweight. His most formidable enemy was pasta. But his pudgy, oversized head and unsophisticated bearing made him endearing.

You could talk to him for five minutes and realize that he reveled in his inspiring story. Fat Tony used to describe himself as a sewer rat because he had toiled in the sewers of the city as a young man. He then worked his way up through the city service department for 30 years.

Tony was proud of his authentic knowledge of the streets, sewers, water lines, wastewater treatment system, and trash collection of this blue-collar town.

In 1975, he was appointed service director of the City of Euclid and no man ever held that post with more knowledge or experience. Tony never earned a college degree, but no engineer could match his uncanny familiarity with the infrastructure of the city. When a water main broke, he knew where the closest junction shut off valve was located without looking at a map.

Tony also knew how to deploy limited resources for maximum results in delivering municipal services from snow removal to unclogging blocked sewers. He took the official motto declaring Euclid the "City of Superior Services" very seriously. This rough-around-the-edges mayor was the Everyman of the Cleveland area political scene. One local paper even speculated that Fat Tony could have his pick of higher elected office beyond mayor.

But that was never a serious consideration. Tony loved being mayor.

Fat Tony was the hardest working man in politics. He never said no to an invitation, from the biggest political rally to a little gathering of the Miller family for Tommy's first communion.

Euclid's two funeral homes, Brickman's and Crobaugh's, saw Tony at least once a week to offer consolation to the bereaved. If he did not know the family of the deceased, Tony did his research before he entered the funeral parlor to express his condolences, sprinkling his remarks with praise for the dearly departed. This was a man with a big heart.

In essence, Tony was popular because he cared about people. They saw Tony as the blue-collar neighbor they wanted to live next door to. Someone who cared about the family of Joe-Bag-of-Doughnuts because Tony himself was Joe-Bag-of-Doughnuts. Tony was unsophisticated but that wasn't a detriment for him. He knew the city inside and out and worked hard. For Euclid citizens, Tony was their guy.

As Mayor, Fat Tony wore suits and ties. But you got the sense that a pair of work boots and canvass gloves were never too far behind.

Fat Tony was beloved. The public's affection for Tony Giunta was reminiscent of the adulation New Yorkers showered on their diminutive Mayor Fiorello LaGuardia in the late 1930's. Both men exuded an old world sense of their Italian heritage and a zest for life. Giunta, like LaGuardia, was trusted because it was clear he wasn't comfortable in board rooms surrounded by the country club set. He was one of us and he would protect our interests.

He was the reason for the Coalition's success in the late 1970s and early 1980s. The brutal domination of the Coalition was hidden in the background.

Tony was the friendly family butcher who handed you your cube steak over the counter in the front of the store. In the backroom of the butcher shop however, cleavers were used for cutting old Bessie into rump roasts and shoulder brisket.

Not a pretty sight. That's why friendly, simple-spoken Fat Tony was in the front.

Mayor Giunta: Man of the people.

Tony was also a soft touch for families in need of a job for the breadwinner. The city budget bloated in part because Tony always found a job for some poor guy down on his luck. Tony helped these people by adding them to the payroll. There were plenty of departments where one more body could be added: streets, wastewater, recreation, parks, housing inspection, and the city golf course.

It may have been bad for municipal finance but it was good politics. Entire families became loyal battalions in Tony's army of campaign workers. People didn't forget they had a good job with good benefits because of Tony. If you hire a man with a large family, you can distribute campaign literature to 5,000 homes over the weekend through that one family alone. Tony made that patronage system work for everybody. Truth is, these hires often brought grateful, hard-working talent into City Hall. Unfortunately, there were many occasions where politics trumped fiscal responsibility.

One of Tony's most notorious hires was Sam Ventura. Sam was a busy man, running his popular barber shop on Shore Center Drive. He was never lacking for customers because city employees knew that Sam was a friend of the mayor. Folks gravitated to his modest storefront location to catch up on city government news, often finding out what was on the horizon long before the papers did. Sam loved the attention and it didn't hurt his business either. Stopping by Sam's was like getting an advance copy of *The Euclid News Journal* weeks before it went to press.

Rocco leaked new ideas to Sam to test public reaction. In what Rocco called "The Barber Poll", Sam would casually mention some new proposal to a long stream of customers and report back to the Law Director. Sam's informal survey was usually dead-on accurate and cost nothing, an efficient barometer of public opinion. Major decisions were frequently put off until the "Man in the Chair" had spoken.

Sam's reconnaissance missions in gathering feedback may have cost the Coalition nothing but it came at a high price for the taxpayers. Sam was rewarded by Giunta with appointment to the lofty post of City Director of Weights and Measures.

Euclid has many stores and gas stations. Any kind of scale, measuring device, or gas pump had to be inspected once a year. The device was then sealed with a sticker that prominently displayed the name of the Mayor with Sam's name in smaller print. As in many communities throughout the United States, these scale and pump inspection stickers promote name recognition for politicians. Apparently this didn't take much of Sam's time. He was always at the barber shop. The policemen carped about the scale inspector who was well-compensated by the government to trim sideburns and order talcum powder.

The worst aspect of the hiring of Sam Ventura was the blatant waste of taxpayer dollars. Sam was carrying out duties already provided by Cuyahoga County free of charge. The county auditor utilized special employees to test the accuracy and reliability of the scales and pumps in every municipality, including Euclid. Giunta paid Sam for services already provided by the county at no cost.

It was ridiculous, but typical for Mayor Tony. After all, Sam was his friend. In addition, Sam was influential in the community. Most importantly, Tony would never part with those brightly-colored, prominently placed stickers constantly reminding us that Mayor Giunta was in charge.

More to the point, Giunta was loyal to a fault. City hall jobs gave him a way to take care of the people who took care of him. It's a practice as old as the hills. The problem is that it isn't always good for the governed. And Tony, partly because he had a big heart and couldn't say no, took political patronage to the extreme, frequently ignoring the cost of fattening the payroll.

The Mayor knew Sam was being paid for a "make-work" job but just assumed that the political advantage would outweigh the political price if someone made an issue of it. Besides, with the Coalition's power, who would be able to make an issue of it?

Things were clicking for Mayor Giunta. The Coalition was riding a wave of success in 1987, and Fat Tony was the champion of the people and the undisputed king of the city. The public loved him and the media left him alone. I was intimidated by his political durability. He had been a part of the Coalition government for over 30 years. Like Lou Gehrig, there was nothing fancy about him, but he always got a hit with men on base. Tony Giunta was the Iron Horse of Northeast Ohio politics.

I pondered ways to pull away the veil of Tony's likability and earthy charisma.

Making sausage is never pretty.

And Fat Tony and the Coalition were making plenty of sausage.

Still, there had to be some political vulnerability. I had to let people see the backroom of the butcher shop. I had to show the people how they were making sausage.

CHAPTER SEVEN

Joe Farrell

JOE FARRELL was a towering giant of an Irishman.

About 6'5" and 290 pounds, Joe was an imposing figure. He had a barrel chest, sort of what you might call a Frankenstein kind of frame, and an athletic bearing. At age 45 in 1987, Joe was in great shape.

In his day, Joe was one hell of a basketball player. If you watch old films from the NBA in the 1950s, the big star was George Mikan, who like Joe Farrell had that ramrod-straight posture. Mikan had below average speed like Farrell, but his rebounding and scoring were superlative because of his athleticism and strength. Joe was George Mikan gone into politics.

That's one of the reasons Joe was so good at his full-time job as Dean of Discipline at St. Joseph High School, an all-boys Catholic institution located in Cleveland right across the street from the far Northwest corner of Euclid.

This City Council job was part-time. Joe Farrell's greatest skill was dealing with young people.

St. Joe's was known as a sports powerhouse especially in football and basketball. Joe Farrell defined St. Joe's in those days. Joe's size and obvious physical power made him the perfect disciplinarian. And Joe wasn't afraid to use his dominating strength to shock some smart aleck into a state of sobriety.

Joe also taught math and social studies at St. Joe's. If some jerk got out of line, Joe could lift the lad off his seat with one hand and throw him across the room.

Chalkboard erasers were known to hit their target against the side of the head of a dozing offender. Joe used to say he loved those old felt erasers because they never left a mark.

The truth is though, Joe wasn't afraid to mete out corporal punishment for misbehaving high school boys.

And for Joe, it worked. You feared Joe Farrell and therefore you behaved. Today Joe would probably get sued.

But back then, parents knew about Joe's intimidating methods. Quite simply, they wanted their boys to behave. If Joe's techniques inspired good behavior, the parents were all for it.

Joe's physicality though, would not have been an effective tool if he didn't also project total love for his students, especially the screw-ups.

Many a wayward youth saw the light after a paddling by Joe was followed by a gentle discussion. The discussion was the key because boys would learn that Joe truly cared for them and understood the challenges of teenage life. After the talk concluded, Joe gave the offender a big bear hug and reminded the young man that he was loved by God.

Joe Farrell: loyal friend and mentor, a force of nature.

Joe's sincere affection for troubled youth was without limit. Joe was blessed with the ability to speak one-on-one with youngsters dealing with drugs, domestic violence, alcohol, or perhaps getting a girl in trouble. Joe never gave up on a kid and that's why parents often took children to see Joe from all over Northeast Ohio. St. Joseph High School paid the salary, but Joe Farrell always had time for disturbed youth, even if they were referred to him from other schools.

Joe's wife Ginny, a beautiful brunette who many years prior had fallen in love with the popular high school basketball star, accepted the fact that a knock on the door in the middle of the night wouldn't be unexpected. Ginny would brew coffee while a parent or wayward youth, desperate for guidance, would take a seat at the kitchen table. Always ending with that embrace that told the recipient everything would be OK because Joe and God himself were on the case.

Joe shaped the lives of thousands of young men, quite a few becoming millionaires, politicians, and professional athletes who attributed their success to one man: Joe Farrell.

Joe Farrell didn't know this paddling was captured on film.
The paddle was customized with airholes to reduce wind resistance.

They will tell you that they were headed down the wrong road until Joe beat them within an inch of their life and then nurtured them lovingly onto the right path.

In essence, Joe's name evoked fatherhood. He told you that he'd stand by you through thick and thin.

And he meant it.

St. Joseph High School was steeped in Catholic religious tradition. Joe therefore was even known to counsel young priests who ran into problems.

I guess you could describe Joe as the father in the story of the Prodigal Son. Joe knew that young men sin but he also knew young men could thrive if someone could convince them that they were forgiven.

Joe never excused the offense and he never tried to set aside punishment. But Joe truly believed in the loving God of the New Testament. Joe had the ability to express God's unlimited capacity to forgive and to love.

One thing about Joe was his language. He was always the picture of decorum at public events. But he also viewed words as mere tools to make a point. Joe was not about to limit his arsenal of tools.

So Joe used all the words available. Including the crude ones. Joe used to say "asshole" and "f---" were just words.

Joe used the word "f---" somewhat liberally in private because he said it fit perfectly so often that no other word in the English language seemed to have the same impact. One of Joe's favorite lines was this: "What about me makes you think I give a f---?"

This usually left the respondent speechless. High school kids and parents found Joe's language part of what made him so real and easy to relate to. Don't let the words bother you, he said. What you should worry about is your family and your relationship with God.

I guess that's why Joe's coarse language never really bothered me. Joe was so sincere in the way he expressed himself that you realized that somehow it all made sense.

Joe loved to help young people and spoke their language. Quite simply, Joe wasn't just loved, he was revered.

One other thing about Joe.

He could drink.

But I never saw him drunk. What I mean is that Joe could drink plenty at one sitting and show no signs of it whatsoever. Few people are able to do such a thing. Joe called it "the gift".

And Joe had it in spades. He once challenged me to a duel.

I would drink vanilla milkshakes and he would drink bourbon, matching each other glass-for-glass. The winner would be declared when someone became too sick or tipsy. I got sick after six milkshakes. Joe drove me home, sober as a judge.

Everybody knew about Joe's ability to drink without getting drunk and it just enlarged the legend. High school boys drink: that's just a reality.

But Joe lectured his young charges to avoid booze because the gift was rarely imparted to anybody.

Perhaps the greatest characteristic of Joe Farrell was that he just did not care what other people thought. He would help kids and fight City Hall, regardless of the cost to himself.

As a result, Joe would cast aside stodgy norms of behavior in favor of an unorthodox approach. Formality and protocol were a waste of time for him. Joe coined "Just Do It" long before Nike came along.

That's the reason he ran for mayor two times. The Coalition was abusive and cruel, so Joe running for mayor was the obvious solution.

One time, Joe invited me to tag along when he scored tickets to the grand opening of the Rock 'n Roll Hall of Fame in Cleveland. The guest of honor was Yoko Ono, the enigmatic wife of John Lennon.

She appeared in black-leather pants, an elegant black and white-checkered jacket, and big sunglasses. Along with three burly bodyguards.

Joe casually handed me a camera and asked me to snap a photo of him with Yoko. I laughed at the absurd idea: he'd never get close.

But before I knew it, Joe was throwing solid picks as if clearing the way for a point-guard to make a layup. The bodyguards were no match for Joe Farrell.

Joe's smile in that photo captures his personality perfectly, displaying his huge toothy grin with a slight gap between the front teeth like David Letterman.

Yoko and Joe

Joe's eyes twinkled, his gigantic arm wrapped around Lennon's widow like they'd both been out painting the town. Ms. Ono has that look of a forced smile (she was still a little stunned, I think) but what a picture!

Joe was a force of nature and those who knew him loved him.

So I told Joe I was running against Fat Tony. He told me I was f-ing crazy. Then he agreed to be my mentor. The fact that I was a Republican and Joe was a Democrat never caused a problem between us. Party labels were irrelevant in Euclid. Besides, I was what was called back then a "progressive" Republican, liberal on social issues but fiscally conservative. What really mattered was that Joe and I agreed on what needed to be done to improve the fortunes of the City of Euclid.

That Giunta was a Democrat like Joe meant nothing. Joe knew evil was at the core of the Coalition in 1987, party politics be damned. Most importantly, Joe and I were joined together in a common cause: the end of the Coalition's ruthless domination of local government.

On countless occasions during all hours he took my calls throughout the campaign. Sometimes I was the knock on the door in the middle of the night. He always had the time and always gave me great advice.

Ending with the trademark comforting bear hug and the same reminder that I was loved by God.

It was going to be a rough ride.

But I had Joe Farrell on my side.

CHAPTER EIGHT

Me

I GUESS IT'S TIME for the reader to learn a few things about me to give some context to what happened in 1987.

I grew up in another suburb on the east side of Cleveland called Cleveland Heights. My dad was a tax lawyer who had worked for the government back in the days of the Depression. His first job was with the Department of Agriculture and he considered himself fortunate to have this employment during the horrible economic times of the early 1930s.

My father was a big fan of Franklin Roosevelt as he rode into the White House on a white horse, and just in the nick of time. Roosevelt implemented scores of new programs that ultimately gave hope to millions of Americans thrown into the depths of despair because of joblessness, hunger, and lack of housing. Roosevelt's "New Deal" saved America from the Depression.

My dad's name was John Kennedy Lynch and he had a special connection to Franklin Roosevelt because a rich uncle had contributed significantly to Roosevelt's campaign coffers.

A phone call from Uncle Matt to the President of the United States led to my father's employment in the Federal Government. This proved to be a lifeline during those dark days. News of food lines, staggering unemployment, and businessmen committing suicide dominated the world of John Kennedy Lynch back then.

My dad made a name for himself during World War II working for the War Department, acquiring for Uncle Sam the real estate necessary for the construction of a little building called The Pentagon. It remains the largest office building in the world to this day.

After the war, my father transferred to the Internal Revenue Service, where he rose in the ranks. His prominence within the IRS eventually led to his leaving the government to open a pretty lucrative practice representing defendants in federal tax matters.

Me helping Dad get ready for my sister's wedding.

My mom was a crusader.

One time my older sister, Mary Kay, barely escaped with her life when the undertow at a beach on Lake Erie took hold of a group of teenagers and wouldn't let go. Mary Kay's best friend drowned. My mother was horrified to learn that a lifeguard was nowhere in sight when the tragedy occurred.

Mom launched a campaign to require lifeguards at public swimming locations. She testified before the state legislature and accumulated thousands of petition signatures. The measure became law.

On another occasion, a World War II submarine docked in Cleveland as a floating museum lost its funding. My mother spearheaded fundraising efforts and the USS Cod continues to receive and educate visitors to this very day. Quite simply, when my mother saw injustice, inequity, or public need, she sprang into action. She was unstoppable.

Mom was also a fantastic artist, churning out oil paintings and sculptures from her little sun room studio on the second floor of our ancient Cleveland Heights colonial. She was in demand as a portrait artist in the Cleveland area. What fond memories I have of lazy days sitting in her huge rocking chair (my feet didn't reach the floor), watching her create a masterpiece working off of nothing but a small photo of her client.

Her favorite subjects apart from her portraits included religious figures, Greek and Roman mythology, and heroes of the American revolution. A winter tradition in Northeast Ohio was Mom's snow sculpture of the Statute of Liberty, ten-feet tall thanks to a step-ladder. A local newspaper photographer trekked to our front yard every year to capture this creation for the features page. The statue was an exact replica. I was in awe.

Mom's Famous Statue of Liberty in the winter of 1965.
That's the artist herself in the white hoody.

I loved going out into the yard as spring approached, Lady Liberty slowly melting into some weird alien life form as her nose fell off and her crown became a collection of disorganized spiky horns. One time, as I stared up in the blazing sun, the torch broke off and landed on my head. Give me your tired, your poor, your huddled masses, and…don't stand too close.

Music was also a huge part of the Lynch family experience. Mom at one point had her own radio show in Washington, D.C., singing many of the famous arias from classic opera. She had an audition with the Metropolitan Opera but chose a career raising ten children instead. Each of the Lynch kids has a recording of Jacqueline Churchill Lynch singing Madame Butterfly as a cherished momento of her awesome talent.

Dad played the violin, even leading a dance band while attending Union college in upstate New York in 1930. This was in the days of Rudy Vallee and megaphones. Dad was also the lead singer. We always joked that the band's name, The Agony Eight, came from the audience's enduring the experience.

*It **was** a wonderful life: The Agony Eight band leader, with fiddle in hand, looks over my shoulder.*

With Mom at the piano and Dad on the violin, Christmas carols rang out from our living room every Christmas Eve, all the offspring in full voice, four-part harmony. Add various cousins and friends and the scene resembled the final moments of *"It's a Wonderful Life."* Even today, it's hard for me to hear "Silent Night" without choking up a little.

I was the ninth of ten children, although my oldest brother John died in infancy of pneumonia. Ten kids seems like a lot, but it was actually pretty common among the Irish and Italian families that dominated St. Ann's Catholic parish in Cleveland Heights in the 1960's.

The Lynch's were Roman Catholic to the core and Mom instilled in us a deep faith. A family crisis, like the time my brother Bob suffered a severe head injury in a motorcycle accident, drove us all to our knees, literally. We would gather in my Dad's library room and kneel, praying the rosary. My Dad would lead the prayers in his rich baritone and you could feel the presence of God listening to our cries for help.

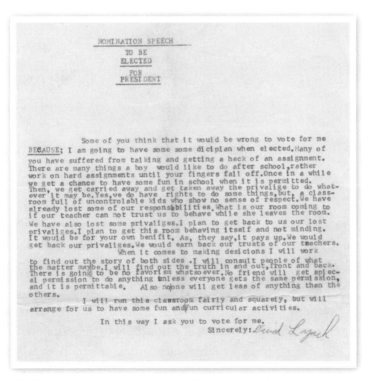

My first campaign speech in pursuit of the fourth grade presidency: I lost.

These experiences made me feel like I could always turn to our heavenly father, especially in the darkest times. During the tough campaign of 1987, I took solace in being able to tap into a spirituality that I viewed as a secret weapon, an inexhaustible resource. Winning for me didn't have to be defined by the results at the ballot box. Winning meant faithfully placing it all in the hands of God. This helped me to relax and gave me a sense of peace in the middle of the storm.

Me in the fifth grade: I was already taking my lumps.

My parents were always active politically, but neither one of them became a candidate for office, except on one occasion. Sometime in the mid-1960s, my father ran for the School Board in the City of Cleveland Heights. I was about eight years old at the time and I can remember going to all the church parking lots, placing leaflets on the windshields of automobiles belonging to worshipers.

My father lost this one and only attempt at political office. I remember learning that some of the Sunday worshipers were irritated to find the leaflets placed under their windshield wipers when they came out of church. Campaigning can be a tricky thing.

I graduated from Cleveland Heights High School in 1975 and followed up in 1979 with a degree from John Carroll University, a Catholic Jesuit college about five minutes from the family home on Fairmount Boulevard. John Carroll is the *alma mater* of the late Tim Russert of Meet the Press fame. Don Shula of the Miami Dolphins is another famous graduate.

After John Carroll, I headed to Georgetown University in Washington, D.C. where I received a law degree in 1982. What a place for a legal education! I could walk to the Supreme Court building from school and observe the oral arguments concerning the most important issues of the day, from abortion to affirmative-action to women's rights.

I was the vocalist delivering the National Anthem at my graduation from Georgetown Law School.

I was hired right out of law school as an Assistant Prosecuting Attorney for the City of Cleveland and began conducting misdemeanor trials almost immediately. It was in this position as a city prosecutor for a major metropolitan municipality that I really learned about politics and people. I was constantly rubbing elbows with judges, public defenders, policemen, city councilmen, and average citizens just trying to make their way through life.

I moved into the City of Euclid after Nancy and I got married in 1982.

Why Euclid?

Only one reason: my wife grew up in Euclid and she insisted that we live there. I knew virtually nothing about this suburb of approximately 68,000 except for the fact that it took about 25 minutes for me to drive there from my parents' home in Cleveland Heights.

In 1983, my wife and I built a new house on a lot that had become available due to the demolition of an old cottage on that site. This was unusual because Euclid was already completely developed at that time.

Nancy and I spent a lot of time overseeing the construction of that little three-bedroom colonial. You would've thought we were designing one of the great museums of Europe. But it was our first home and we were thrilled.

After we moved in, life for us settled down and we began to take our place in the community, Nancy pursuing her teaching career while I focused on various misdemeanor prosecutions in the big city downtown.

Misdemeanors are not as serious as felonies, but I took these cases very seriously. I think I irritated some of the defense lawyers because I completely threw myself into conducting these trials. I developed a reputation as someone who was overdoing things. I used to spend hours going to crime scenes and interviewing witnesses, something very few of the municipal prosecutors bothered to do.

The defense attorneys may have hated this, but the police officers loved it. I formed lots of long and lasting relationships with policemen who to this very day are my good friends.

Inner-city police work is unbelievably challenging and the average citizen has no appreciation for what it takes to keep our streets safe, especially when politicians frequently challenge the budgets in safety departments. I received an important education in government during those days as a prosecutor.

In any case, I noticed that the curbs in the neighborhood of my new home in Euclid needed attention. I contacted City Hall and received a very reasoned explanation that the city's capital improvement program did not include curb replacement in our area until a couple of more years down the line. I understood the explanation, but I wasn't satisfied. I spoke to our councilman, George Carson, who merely repeated the viewpoint of the city administration.

I decided to attend a few of the City Council meetings in 1984 and that's where I had my first exposure to Giunta, Rocco, Chukayne, and the Euclid Independent Coalition party.

Carson, my own Ward Three Councilman, was a very affable and articulate representative. He worked for the local phone company on a full-time basis and was also known as a bass player in a popular polka band. But there was no doubt that like the other coalition councilmen, he had been given a program to follow and there was no way he was going to buck that system.

Grainy campaign photo of George Carson and Mayor Giunta.

I decided to run against George in the election of November 1985. I knocked on every door in Ward 3, and the experience was pretty exciting for a 28-year-old kid who had only recently moved into the city.

As you can imagine, the Coalition, because of my recent arrival in town, described me as a carpetbagger. I found this amusing because a carpetbagger is someone who comes in to take advantage of people, only to disappear, leaving destruction in his wake.

Nancy gave birth to our first child, Scott, in July of 1985. I told the public that I represented the future of Euclid with my new young family, hoping to build up the community. The residents of Ward 3 seemed to agree with me.

There was one other part of that campaign, however, that should have given me pause. George Carson and the Coalition kept referencing the fact that I had grown up in Cleveland Heights and had attended Cleveland Heights High School.

At first, I didn't quite understand why this was constantly mentioned in my opponent's literature. Joe Farrell explained it to me .

Cleveland Heights was a suburban community that was well known for and in fact publicized its diversity. Instead of fighting the influx of African-Americans trying to escape the difficulties of inner-city life, Cleveland Heights became nationally recognized for developing programs to welcome residents of color and to peacefully integrate the community.

These efforts in Cleveland Heights were a rousing success and everybody knew that Cleveland Heights stood as a beacon for tolerance.

For this reason, the Coalition wanted everybody to know that I grew up in Cleveland Heights and had graduated from a high school where black and white students studied together. It was a shorthand way of warning people that David Lynch represented the influx of minorities.

"Don't vote for Dave Lynch because he's from Cleveland Heights. We all know what that means."

Despite this disgusting effort to derail my shot at the Ward 3 council seat, I was elected in a pretty close race. Those interested in the future of Euclid prevailed over those who thought it was important to keep the city a white enclave.

It was just a few days later in November of 1985 that Frank Chukayne summoned me to the fateful meeting in his office I describe in the first chapter of this book.

CHAPTER NINE

The First of Two Stories

IN CHAPTER EIGHT, I gave you some background about me so you could understand the context of this amazing political tale. Here in chapters nine and ten, I present two impactful events that made a deep imprint on my psyche that I think might give an even greater insight into what shaped me into the person who lived through this story. It's what a news reporter might refer to as "deep background".

The first event took place when I was only seven years old.

That's when I lost my best bud Brian Doyle.

Here's what happened.

Brian and I both attended St. Ann School at Coventry and Cedar Roads in Cleveland Heights.

Sometime in 1963 we bumped into each other walking home a fair distance east of our elementary school. We bonded immediately.

Brian's hopes and dreams. My hopes and dreams. We discussed girls, the scary nuns (Sister St. John, the principal from hell, terrified us), the foibles of our classmates, and the finer points of bloodball. Bloodball was a ruthless keepaway game played during lunch recess on the asphalt parking lot of our school.

When our routes home finally diverged, Brian went his way and I went mine. Day ended.

We never went to each other's houses, so our families, I think, never knew about this friendship.

But there was no doubt, regardless of what our families knew, Brian Doyle was my best friend in the world.

He knew me and I knew him.

We both had lots of brothers and sisters and we knew that growing up together at St. Ann's held the promise of great times together, loyal friends through thick and thin.

Brian Doyle: My best pal could really pull off the bow tie look.

We looked forward to the spring of 1964 because it meant baseball in the schoolyard and outdoor gym class.

Suddenly, Brian wasn't there.

Our teacher announced that Brian Doyle had drowned visiting a hotel while his family was traveling near Columbus, Ohio. My soulmate was gone.

I wanted to tell the teachers, my classmates, and my family that I had lost my alter ego.

But I was a second grader.

They didn't have grief counselors for us back then.

It seemed that my friendship with Brian was a secret he would take to the grave.

The whole second grade went to the funeral. I blended in with all the rest.

Anonymously shuffled through the service, quietly, in agony.

I imagined Brian's fear in his last seconds and shared those moments with him tearfully, he in the arms of Jesus while I plodded along, alone.

I remember closing my eyes and talking to him again. Life moves forward, but Brian makes himself known to me on a regular basis, creeping into my consciousness and into my prayers.

What's the impact on young folks when they lose a friend?

Massive.

Especially if that friend is Brian Doyle.

I cherish those memories.

And I look forward to a reunion in heaven.

That dismissal bell rings and we're bounding eastward on Stillman Road, adventures along the way.

A friendship to be fulfilled, together, finally.

Life went on after Brian. But that sense of loneliness and melancholy stayed with me and made me appreciate relationships with people. I knew from experience at a very young age that they could be gone in an instant.

CHAPTER TEN

The Second Story

IN A DARK BOX, locked away in my memory, pushed into a corner of my past that I rarely visit, is a recollection that despite the passage of time, remains disturbingly vivid.

I tremble as I write this.

As a young law student, I interned with the police prosecutor's office in Cleveland one summer. It was common practice for a hopeful future prosecutor to spend the night with the police during third shift.

These days, many citizens have such an opportunity with police departments as part of a "Citizens Police Academy".

I was assigned to ride with two seasoned cops named Jim Simone and Dave Sumskis.

Patrolman Dave Sumskis (left) and Jim Simone (right): America's best crime fighting team.

Most of the night was spent responding to a couple of neighborhood disputes and a hardware store break-in. The three of us were stopped at a diner for a quick cup of coffee when the dispatcher radioed that there were reports of gunfire at a home just a few blocks away.

Just like in the movies, we dashed to the cruiser and were at top speed on the way to the residence in question.

What we found stops my heart cold to this very day.

A young man in his thirties, faced with a myriad of personal problems, took a high-powered rifle and killed his girlfriend, his brother and sister, and then shot himself in the head.

The carnage was all over the front porch and the front yard, a body here and then two more over there.

On the front sidewalk near the driveway was the poor tormented perpetrator, a victim of his inability to get help in a moment of crisis.

His body was intact but his head was not.

A portion of his head, the part containing his face from the upper lip to his forehead was laying on the sidewalk, bloody. It was like some kind of macabre Picasso painting, you know, where parts of faces appear in different places on the canvas.

This face-bearing part of his head looked out into the world.

The eyes were wide open and staring out in a frightening look.

My mind, against my will, took a digital snapshot of that part of that face and it has haunted me ever since.

Those eyes.

They reflected a sense of desperation, hopelessness, and abandonment.

I went home that night and couldn't sleep. Many weeks went by before I could begin to tuck that vision far enough away into my subconscious before peaceful sleep would come to me.

What did I really see that night? I'm not sure. The image is so disturbing that it's reappearance in my mind's eye prevents explanation, emotion overwhelming analysis.

Alone. Abandoned. Perhaps a lonely road to Calvary with the heaviest of crosses.

Hug your kids, hug your whole family, hug your dog, and live your life with gentle love.

There is horrible anger and hopelessness about. Let completely gentle love permeate your life in all things, especially with those close to you.

Being right is never more important than being loving and trusting in God.

After law school, I began my first full-time job in the law in that same City of Cleveland Prosecutor's office.

Officer Dave Sumskis died of heart disease a few years later. Jim Simone went on to become the most decorated police officer in America and I had the privilege of working with him on many cases. Simone's incredible career is beautifully chronicled in a recent book release called "Badge 357" by author Robert Sberna. I still see Simone every now and then. He always gives me a warm knowing smile.

He knows that we are bound together by that moment and by that face.

A face that became a memory that just won't go away.

CHAPTER ELEVEN

Campaign Begins

UP UNTIL THE END of August 1987, things were strangely quiet and uneventful. I was flying under the radar. The Coalition did not think I was a threat.

There are couple of reasons for this. First of all, the Coalition ran a poll in the summer of 1987. It seems that even the overconfident Coalition accepted the idea that campaign technology could help them run the machine.

A survey led them to believe that Fat Tony was unbeatable. The telephone call made to the homes of registered voters showed Tony Giunta likely to win because Tony had a 64% approval rating. In addition, Tony held a three-to-one edge over candidate Lynch in terms of voters who knew their preference. It would take a miracle for anyone to beat Tony with numbers like that.

Secondly, even though I was the only person that had pulled blank petitions to become a potential candidate, the Coalition didn't think I was going to actually run for mayor.

The filing deadline for submitting the requisite signed petitions for the November election was August 15, just three months prior to the election. Euclid has no primaries so having sufficient petition signatures guarantees you a spot on the general election ballot.

That's what sunk Joe Farrell and Mark Jochum years earlier: multiple opponents just split any anti-Coalition vote to the extent there was one. Because the filing deadline was so late in August, and so close to the general election, the Coalition never realized I was actually running hard from February all the way up until the date I filed my petitions in mid-August.

So for the Fat Tony machine, they saw the campaign as beginning in August of 1987.

This was reinforced by the fact that I did not circulate one piece of campaign literature until after the filing deadline. The Coalition just didn't believe anyone was really running against Tony until my petitions appeared at the Board of Elections on the last day for filing in August.

This lack of outward signs of a campaign lulled the old Coalition into a sense of complacency up until that moment.

But I knew the secret truth. I had completed about 70% of my campaign work on the day that I filed.

You see, I knew I wouldn't have the money for mass mailings and glossy campaign flyers. Those glitzy political tri-folds that were the key to Coalition victories over the years were very expensive.

These Coalition pieces were also brilliant, featuring Euclid as the ideal patch of America with neighborhoods surrounded by parks and ball diamonds. The photography was stunning, with full color in the days before the world went digital. At a time when newer suburbs were sprawling out further from the core city, Euclid was lovingly described as a safe and secure community with real sidewalks as the pedestrian highway between neighbors who cared for and knew one another.

Newer developments in far-flung distant outer ring suburbs had large lots, great distances between homes, and zero sidewalks. Euclid was a place where you could enjoy a weekend without using your car, lounging on the back porches and patios of neighbors on your own block. Shopping and informal dining was within a walk or a bike ride.

These beautifully designed releases made it seem as if it were 1956. The Eisenhower era would last forever if you continued to support your Coalition party and Anthony J. Giunta.

And no candidate could ever outspend the Coalition. They had money to spare from the contractors that benefited from City Hall corruption.

So I launched a campaign that began in February of 1987 that cost me no more than $50 for the business cards printed with my name identifying me as a candidate for mayor. Then tramping through the cold snowy winter of Northeast Ohio, I began knocking on doors sometime right after Valentine's Day.

Lynch for Mayor campaign photo.

In fact, I began a crusade to do something no one had ever done. I was going to knock on every door of every registered voter in the City of Euclid.

And with most of the door knocking quietly accomplished by the time I filed my petitions, the foundation of my campaign was already in place just as the Coalition was sharpening its knives for the political street fight that was brewing. Those doorstep conversations with Euclidians, according to the poll, didn't guarantee me a victory. But it did give citizens an awareness of me. If I could use those last months of the campaign to elevate awareness into political support, I might have a chance.

I needed issues to energize the electorate. I found a few, but effectively conveying them to the public was another matter.

Little David searched for a smooth flat rock for hurling at giants.

CHAPTER TWELVE

Cemented Relationships

FAT TONY AND THE COALITION always had campaigns lavishly funded by contractors doing business with the city. To reward this support, a lot of techniques were used to circumvent state laws requiring the bidding of municipal contracts.

A common way around this involved the declaration of an emergency. A state statute exempted construction contracts from bidding requirements where dire circumstances were such that there was no time to write specifications, publish them, accept bids, evaluate the bids, and formally award the contract.

For the Coalition, they merely stretched the definition of an emergency to give city contracts to companies willing to reciprocate by joyfully donating to Tony's campaign.

After a water main break left a portion of a roadway in shambles, the Coalition awarded an emergency contract to repave the entire mile stretch of a five lane thoroughfare. This practice was par for the course in the Coalition government.

However, the Coalition often did award contracts to the lowest bidder after a formal bidding process. It's just that Fat Tony had discovered a way to make sure that his friends were always the lowest bidder.

The Coalition practically invented the concept of the "combined bid" contract. It was a brilliant scheme because it never failed. The key was collusion between the Mayor and the favored contractor so they could fix the bids in the contract. Here's the way it worked.

One of Tony's favorite contractors was the Dominic Calabrese Cement Company. Tony could arrange for Calabrese to win the cement contract as long as Calabrese got the inside scoop on how to bid.

The city would publish a request for bids on a contract requiring bids on three different cement requirements. The city would ask for bids on cement curbs, cement sidewalks, and cement driveway aprons. All three types of cement work were combined in the bid specifications, the city to order quantities for each item after the award of the bid.

The incoming combined bids might look something like this:

Cement Bid Summary

Type of Work	Calabrese	Company A	Company B
Sidewalk	$12	$8	$7
Curbs	$8	$5	$4
Aprons	$4	$13	$14
Total Combined Bid	**$24**	**$26**	**$25**

In the above scenario, Calabrese is awarded the contract because his combined bid total is the lowest of all three bidders. But notice Calabrese is only lowest because his bid for driveway aprons is remarkably low in comparison to the other companies. In the curbs and sidewalks portion, Calabrese is actually more expensive than the others.

Using the chart of bids as included here however, Calabrese wins the bid and accepts the lucrative cement contract.

But the fix was in.

The city government, it turns out, has no need for driveway aprons that year. For the annual contract, the Coalition government orders only sidewalks and curbs from Calabrese.

The taxpayers pay the highest bid rate for sidewalks and curbs. Tony's friend makes a fortune. What a coincidence that the item for which Calabrese bid a ridiculously low price is just not in demand that year!

Essentially, the award of city contracts was a form of fundraising for the political machine.

In July of 1986, a brave cement contractor went to the newspapers to complain about the favoritism shown The Dominic Calabrese Cement Company. John Allega, a competitor of Calabrese, explained the combined bid process designed to benefit the chosen few. The story published in the *Euclid News Journal* hardly caused a ripple. It should have resulted in an indictment.

Who could compete when contractor friends like Calabrese were falling over themselves to write checks for Tony's re-election effort?

What made me nervous was the realization that there were powerful businessmen out there who had a vested interest in defeating me or maybe even something more diabolical. Big money has a way of making evil men carry out evil deeds.

I didn't want to go swimming in Lake Erie wearing cement overshoes.

CHAPTER THIRTEEN

ROCCO

IF THE COALITION LEADERS I've described so far seem like cartoon stereotypes, you might find my description of Pat Rocco a little hard to swallow.

But the evil heart of the Coalition was embodied by Pat Rocco, the Law Director of the City of Euclid, and the most feared man along the Lake Erie coastline.

Rocco had suffered from childhood polio, so he required leg braces and a cane to force his legs to move. He used his upper body strength to swing his hips in a powerful motion that forced the weakened legs to pendulum forward, ready to take the next step. His torso, as a result, was quite muscular, and he was in great physical condition, despite his handicap.

Rocco had dark deep set eyes, olive skin, and beautiful wavy black hair with silver trim. He exuded an energetic aura. You could sense it when you were around him. But that energy, one could also feel, was a dark energy. There was something frightening about him.

He reminded me of that feeling you get when you are on the edge of a tall cliff. The view is spectacular and terrifying all at the same time.

Rocco's ascendance to the top rung of power within the Coalition occurred because of a vacuum of leadership within the organization. Mayor Sims began to develop health problems in the late 1960's. I'm sure the difficulties experienced by his friend Judge Robert Steele didn't help things. Sims retired in 1970, leaving Council President Harry Knuth to finish out his term. Knuth was elected to his own term as Mayor in 1971. Knuth, however, while a competent legislator, was not adept at administration.

He lacked the drive and passion to be an effective leader. As a result, the Coalition began to drift somewhat. The Coalition was a powerful steed, but someone needed to take the reins.

In steps Patrick Ralph Rocco. He had insinuated himself into the Euclid law department a few years earlier, and now he was poised to take charge. Knuth appointed Rocco Law Director in December of 1973.

He was now the *de facto* leader of the Coalition as he provided the ideas and the plans for long term growth of the Coalition political organization. Rocco was relatively young, only age 43, when he was asked to head the law department. But he was dynamic, determined, talented, and articulate, impressing the rest of the Coalitionists.

Rocco in charge at his desk at his private office.

Rocco was the strongest Coalition leader to come along since Ken Sims. Those were big shoes to fill, but it was generally acknowledged that the torch had been passed. The real power in the city now resided in the law department, not in the Mayor's office. But with Rocco's firm hand guiding it, the Coalition carried forward with one success after another at the ballot box.

Rocco had his own style. Like Chukayne, he clenched his teeth on an ever-present unlit cigar. But he preferred to operate mostly in secrecy and in the background. He would often take the microphone at Coalition political events, but to the public the Mayor was the real leader and Rocco wanted it this way. In his own time, he would design a method that might allow him to step out from the shadows, but that would come later.

Rocco conducted affairs at his private law office on Euclid Avenue, showing up at City Hall only one day a week. This helped keep his machinations under wraps as virtually everything at City Hall was considered a public record, subject to scrutiny.

No record of appointments or notes of meetings were required to be kept at Rocco's private law office, however. All the big political deals were formulated behind those closed doors on Euclid Avenue.

It was Rocco who ended the mayoral reign of the two mayors who followed Ken Sims: Harry Knuth and Tony Sustarsic.

Knuth quit politics because Rocco turned on him after he appointed Rocco the Law Director. Rocco found Knuth always vacillating instead of immediately embracing Rocco's ideas. Rocco had no patience for this and "suggested" to Knuth that it was time to move on after only one elected term in office as mayor.

Knuth was bitter as he left government forever, the Coalition clearly under the control of the domineering Law Director. Knuth had begun his career as a councilman elected in 1937 as part of the original Ken Sims contingent.

Now he left office tearfully. Rocco was no Ken Sims and Knuth was struck with the realization that the Rocco-led Coalition lacked the moral character of the original edition. Rocco then asked cabinet member Tony Sustarsic to take up the mantle and run for Mayor under the Coalition banner. Sustarsic was elected in 1975 in a rousing victory over Joe Farrell in the first of Farrell's two bids for mayor.

Not surprisingly, Sustarsic then became too popular for Rocco's taste. The Mayor's popularity made it more difficult for Rocco to control him.

Mayor Tony Sustarsic had chiseled good looks reminiscent of the actor James Arness who played Marshall Matt Dillon on the old "Gunsmoke" television series. Increasing the political potency of Mayor Sustarsic was his heroism during World War II. He lost a leg during the Battle of The Bulge.

Add to all of this a charismatic charm and anyone could see that Mayor Sustarsic was a force to be reckoned with. Euclid truly loved its handsome favorite son who had sacrificed a limb to save the world from the Nazi peril.

Unfortunately, Sustarsic made the mistake of occasionally questioning Rocco's judgment. Not smart.

Rocco announced that Sustarsic's heart ailment would prevent him from running for re-election for a second term as the Coalition Mayor. Mayor Sustarsic knew he was checkmated.

Rocco, acting in concert with Chukayne, controlled the troops: the city workers. In addition, Rocco could destroy Sustarsic with legal rulings that would decimate the Mayor's authority at City Hall. So Sustarsic rode off into the sunset and Rocco pegged Tony Giunta, the popular service director who had worked his way up the government totem pole, to become the next Mayor.

Some inside City Hall speculated that Rocco had something on Sustarsic. Regardless, Sustarsic lived another 30 years in relatively good health. But Rocco wanted a new Mayor and Tony Giunta was the perfect candidate. Rocco finally got what he wanted: a puppet for the master puppeteer.

Giunta and the handsome Mayor Sustarsic.

Rocco was the mastermind pulling all the strings. Fat Tony was the titular leader. The Mayor only carried out the strategies designed by Rocco.

What was unsettling about Rocco was that he always had a scowl on his face. One could conclude that he was always angry. Sometimes it seemed he was like Ahab, looking for revenge against the great white whale that crippled him. Those opposing the Coalition were made to feel like they were that white whale, subject to a harpoon thrust by the city's Law Director at any time.

Everyone feared Rocco because he was a smoldering volcano that could erupt at any moment, causing some poor slob to lose his job at City Hall.

Rocco's anger may have made him Ahab but his evil overtones also made him the Darth Vader of City Hall. Rocco was known for issuing legal opinions that ended careers on a whim. No one dared cross him. Rocco had a mysterious hold over the elected officials in the Coalition government. Even Fat Tony feared him.

Rocco carried his physical impairment as part of his mystique. Just as Darth Vader's breathing helmet added to his terrible threatening aspect, the snapping of Rocco's walking stick against the floor enhanced the air of the demonic that surrounded him. Occasionally he would point his cane at someone who had fallen short of expectations, squint his eyes, and pronounce sentence.

That's when you knew you were dead, figuratively speaking, or at least in terms of your future at City Hall. He exerted his power freely and always to his advantage.

He's the one who suggested to Mayor Sims that the governor should be urged to appoint Coalition water boy Robert Niccum to the vacancy created by the departure of Judge Robert Steele. He's the one who told Fat Tony who to hire for the most sensitive leadership positions at City Hall. He's the one who filled out the dance card determining the Coalition candidates for City Council.

Rocco was ruthless and at age 57 he was at the apex of his power in 1987. With the exception of the 1985 Council race that saw me defeat George Carson, the armor of the Coalition seemed impenetrable.

Rocco wanted to keep it that way. He planned Fat Tony's re-election strategy and he didn't want anyone getting in the way.

No one had more at stake in Fat Tony's reelection than Rocco. Here's why.

Rocco had quietly put into place the mechanism to fulfill his own megalomaniacal ambitions when he had the City Council place a charter change before the voters in 1985. The city's charter was amended almost without anyone noticing.

Here's the way the charter was changed: If the Mayor were to step down, the Law Director would become the Mayor. Since its formation, the charter of the City of Euclid contained a line of succession to pass power from the Mayor to the City Council President if the Mayor retired or died while in office. After all, at least the City Council President was a person who had been elected by the people.

But Rocco, the power behind the throne for so long, had at last orchestrated a way to place himself enticingly close to having the throne itself. The charter thus altered, he was now first in line to succeed Mayor Giunta if he were to step down. The plan designed by

Rocco was obvious. The re-election of Tony Giunta in 1987 would be followed by Giunta's retirement mid-term. Knuth and Sustarsic had been relieved of duty by the Law Director just a few years earlier. Soon it would be Mayor Giunta's turn and poor Fat Tony couldn't see what was in store for him.

My favorite photo of the leadership of the evil empire:
Giunta gladhands after defeating Farrell while Rocco ponders future conquests.

Rocco would finally wear the crown in the kingdom he controlled. Rocco could taste it. It was so close.

And I stood in his way.

Did I fear him? Yes, I did.

Rocco made my blood run cold.

CHAPTER FOURTEEN

Crazy Judge

ROBERT J. NICCUM got a call one day in 1969 from The Coalition. They wanted Niccum to be the new judge of the Euclid Municipal Court. Because one single judge had jurisdiction over the entire City of Euclid, it was a powerful post.

It was also a good source of patronage jobs. The judge appointed all the assistant clerks of court, probation officers, secretaries, bailiffs, public defenders, and other jobs associated with judicial administration.

The previous judge, Robert Steele, was a Coalition guy who lost his seat because he was under suspicion for murdering his wife. It is a testament to the Coalition's power and its almost hypnotic control of the citizenry that the Steele incident never slowed down the Coalition momentum. Only the most powerful political force could survive the dirty details surrounding the Steele murder.

The married Steele had been patronizing prostitutes for years when he served as the president of the Euclid Independent Coalition Party. After donning the judicial robes, he began a torrid love affair with a secretary working in the clerk's office in his court.

An intruder crept up on Mrs. Steele one night, shooting her in the head while she slept at the Steele's Euclid home on Miami Drive in a beautiful housing development called Indian Hills. It seemed like a simple burglary gone bad. Unfortunately for Judge Steele, the assassins hired to eliminate his wife had long records and a tendency to blab after a few too many pints of Guinness. The truth eventually surfaced, with the killers testifying against Steele in return for reduced sentences.

Judge Robert Steele breaks down at a news conference four days after his wife was found murdered in their bedroom. A persistent FBI agent proved that Steele was the mastermind behind the crime.

Soon after the shooting but long before his conviction, Judge Steele was forced to resign as the public began to pick up on the stories of his indiscretions. Most Euclidians felt deep down that Steele was guilty of homicide.

The Coalition leaders said "Oh well" and then promptly picked Steele's replacement, calling the Governor with instructions to appoint their man, Robert Niccum, to the vacancy. Governor James A. Rhodes obliged. After all, even down at the state capital in Columbus, everyone knew that the power in Euclid lay with The Coalition.

Bob Niccum was the perfect Coalition candidate for judge because he was willing to do what he was told. Niccum served as the prosecutor in Judge Steele's courtroom and Niccum loved his judge. This didn't hurt Niccum because after all, Niccum was Coalition all the way.

Niccum had the personality of Barney Fyfe. He was a man of few words and was delighted to be the lawyer who served the great

Robert Steele. A few whispered that Niccum knew something about the murder because Niccum worked with Steele closely every day. Niccum's selection by the Coalition, however, was all that was needed to elevate him to the position held by his beloved mentor who had fallen from grace.

Niccum also had a strange quirk.

He stuttered.

Badly.

Coalition leaders assigned drivers to get Niccum to campaign events in the judicial race that soon followed after his appointment to fill the vacancy on the bench. They had to practically shove him out to the podium to deliver campaign speeches.

Niccum speaking at campaign events demonstrated that he had nerves of jello. It was disastrous. The more he was forced to speak publicly, the more nervous he became. The more nervous he became, the more he stuttered. The Coalition wasn't worried. They knew that even if Mickey Mouse ran on the Coalition ticket, he'd soon be wielding the judicial gavel.

They were right.

Ken Sims was by this time in the waning days of his career as Mayor but he was still a legend. He very publicly endorsed the meek and mild Bob Niccum. That's all he needed, despite receiving bar association ratings well below his opponent's.

Niccum prevailed, along with the other Coalition candidates. Lawyers who knew Bob Niccum scratched their heads, but they chalked it up to the *Peter Principle*: people rise to their level of incompetence.

Of course, these lawyers did not know the Coalition. It could do no wrong.

Once Niccum was elected to the post in his own right, he began to develop more confidence in conducting the substantial docket of cases in his courtroom. In fact, some described it as a metamorphosis.

This mealy-mouthed nervous wreck became a new man as he climbed up onto the bench to judge his fellow citizens. On the bench, his speech impediment was virtually undetectable. He issued forth with a firm baritone.

It was startling.

After he left the courtroom and went into his chambers, the stuttering returned. Niccum putting on the robes and taking his seat on the bench each morning was the equivalent of Clark Kent stepping into a phone booth. Clark Kent returned after the day's judicial proceedings concluded.

In fact, Niccum was so powerful in his demeanor that he began to develop quite a reputation as a judge. Unfortunately for those who went before him, Niccum exerted that power to the point of abuse.

After about two years on the bench, Niccum was tagged with the moniker that follows him to this very day: Stick'em Niccum.

Niccum believed in dressing people down, especially those he didn't like. He seemed to enjoy the misery of others, so he always made it worse. Speeding tickets were consistently at the maximum fine. Everything was at the maximum fine.

And you better not give him any guff because then you were in contempt of court. That meant jail. Niccum loved sending people to jail.

Some lawyers gave up handling cases in his courtroom because they knew Niccum regarded all as guilty. Barristers used to hope for a lower-level felony charge instead of a first-degree misdemeanor in Euclid. Low-level felonies were sent downtown to the Common Pleas Court in Cleveland where probation was almost automatic for first offenders. The same offenders charged with only a misdemeanor would always go to jail in front of Niccum.

Imagine an attorney trying to convince the prosecutor to charge his client with felony breaking and entering instead of misdemeanor trespassing.

Only in Euclid before the Honorable Robert F. Niccum. Niccum struck fear into the hearts of those headed for his court.

Especially if you were black.

This is the most insidious aspect of his judgeship. Niccum saw himself as the protector of the racial purity of the realm. He relished his reputation in the white community as the one holding the line against integration.

African-Americans got the message: stay out of Euclid because any infraction meant facing Niccum.

And he would make you pay. Frequently you paid by surrendering your freedom to the accommodations of the Euclid jail. Niccum wanted everyone to know that Euclid was not a place for black people to hang out. And they better not move there.

Niccum was revered in the all-white neighborhoods that pondered the potential of African-American neighbors on the block. Niccum became somewhat of a folk hero for racists throughout the country when he tossed a man out of his courtroom for wearing a religious cap as part of his Muslim practice. The ensuing lawsuit didn't bother Niccum. He enjoyed the publicity.

Stories of his harsh treatment of blacks solidified his stature in the white community. Toya Johnson and her husband Harold had no criminal record when they placed their 11-month old son in a new stroller for sale at a discount store.

Despite the fact that they never even tried to leave the store with the item, they were charged with theft. Niccum told a reporter that it became a crime the moment the baby was placed in the pram, implying that the baby's black skin somehow contaminated the little carriage.

Cleveland Plain Dealer writer Joe Dirck excoriated the Judge in a now famous column. Niccum was pleased to be the object of this kind of criticism. This enhanced his reputation with voters terrified by the prospect of black people in Euclid.

In an unusually courageous move, black tenants in a Euclid apartment building staged a rent strike against a white landlord who had refused to correct unhealthy conditions. The units in question housed the few African-Americans living in the city. Represented by legendary civil rights attorney Avery Friedman, minority families marched into Niccum's court to place their rent in escrow in accordance with a tenant rights statute recently passed by the state legislature.

Depositing rent in the court would break the back of the white landlord, essentially forcing him to rectify the building code violations in order to gain release of the embargoed funds. Niccum detested Friedman as a provocateur, stirring up trouble on the plantation. The judge refused to accept the money, saying he lacked the forms necessary to accept tenant rental fees, despite the mandatory state law. Although Niccum finally capitulated under threat of a Federal court order, his stiff opposition to black renters earned him high marks among the white majority.

Attorney Avery Friedman battled Niccum's racism.
Today he is a featured legal analyst on CNN.

So despite the unsteady twit unsure of himself off the bench, the Coalition had stumbled into yet another success. On the bench, Niccum was a force to be reckoned with.

Niccum won awards for efficiency, not justice.

Niccum's vicious treatment of black offenders grew to mythical status throughout the State of Ohio. Niccum loved it. Stick'em Niccum was a rock star among segregationists.

Niccum scoffed at the constitutional presumption of innocence, ordering bizarrely high bonds to keep the accused in jail until the day of trial. This was what Niccum privately called his "pre-conviction sentencing."

Niccum's rulings were occasionally reviewed by the Court of Appeals but he didn't care. He was a modern day Judge Roy Bean.

He, along with Rocco, Fat Tony, and Chukayne, ran the town for the benefit of well-behaved white people. Everybody else could go to hell as far as he was concerned.

Politically, this was a winning formula.

Niccum also developed an especially tough attitude toward drunk drivers. Mothers Against Drunk Driving (MADD) praised him for his tenacious resistance to defense attorneys trying to prove the innocence of alleged offenders.

But Niccum's famous tirades against drunk drivers obscured his true hypocrisy: Niccum had a serious drinking problem. Euclid patrolmen knew the truth. Euclid police frequently drove him home after he was found passed out behind the wheel. Niccum was a tough pro-police law-and-order guy, so the police chief had put out the word: take care of our judge.

Police assigned to court duty were frequently appalled to observe the high-handed attitude of Niccum as he railed against drivers who exceeded the legal blood-alcohol limit. Niccum didn't care. He knew that his power and popularity, like Fat Tony's, were trump cards that could win any election in the City of Euclid.

So he continued to play the role of the tough on crime jurist despite the reality that he himself was one of our city's worst offenders. He believed in the rule of law only as long as it permitted him to abuse blacks and polish his image as the *Great White Hope*.

As part of the opposition to the Coalition, I knew none of my clients would stand a chance in his courtroom. I would have to campaign hard and just stay out of his way.

At least that was my plan.

Motivation

ONE OF THE STARTLING THINGS about the Coalition the first few months of 1987 was their inability to set aside their arrogant attitude in favor of making the smart move.

In March of that year, the Coalition lost one of its most popular political leaders. Councilman Ed Sustarsic, brother of former Coalition Mayor Tony Sustarsic, passed away after battling cancer for several months.

Ed Sustarsic had consistently been the top vote-getter among the Coalition councilmen for years. He had a real down-to-earth sense about him, never mincing words, always expressing himself very directly.

Of course, he was loyal in his support of Fat Tony, but that didn't stop him from voicing his impatience with citizens wasting Council's time with some lamebrain idea.

He was popular because he had a reputation for focusing on the basics of local government such as public safety and trash collection. New federal programs coming out of Washington were a distraction as far as he was concerned, especially since those programs usually included requirements for the equitable treatment of minorities.

It wasn't unusual for Ed to call someone an "asshole" right in the middle of a public meeting. Council President Mike Kosmetos would feign irritation when he heard Sustarsic issue forth with this kind of language. Sustarsic was clearly out of order with this lack of decorum. But Kosmetos knew that this was part of Ed's persona. Ed's behavior on the council floor increased his popularity. As Council President, Kosmetos was expected to be the point man in shepherding the Coalition agenda to final passage. He knew that the former mayor's brother was key to the expanding fortunes of the Coalition. Ed's sailor vocabulary was therefore tolerated.

But now with Ed Sustarsic's untimely demise, someone had to be appointed to complete the little over 18 months left in the popular Councilman's unfinished term.

It didn't take long.

The Coalition caucused and publicly pretended to contemplate five candidates who expressed interest in appointment to the vacancy. The appointment went to Jerry Sustarsic, Ed's nephew and the son of the former Mayor. Jerry was a draftsman working for an engineering firm doing business with the city.

But he had a name that was magic in the City of Euclid and from a political standpoint, appointing one Sustarsic to take the place of another made all the sense in the world. Soon thereafter, however, the Coalition was faced with a little problem. The problem would've remained insignificant if the Coalition had exercised some common sense and restraint.

Eight Councilmen divvied up the chairmanships of the eight standing committees of the City Council. Mark Jochum and Joe Farrell each were permitted committee chairmanships under the system, although they were never given the helm of any of the important committees, such as finance or safety. Ed Sustarsic's death meant that the Wastewater Treatment Committee was without a chairman. The committee did not meet very often and it had traditionally been viewed as a trivial body.

However, I had recently been making waves about the operation of the city's wastewater treatment plant and the fact that the smokestacks at the city's wastewater sludge incinerator had been malfunctioning, causing pollution issues. I had even discovered that the smokestacks lacked the required EPA licensing and registration. This embarrassed Rocco and Giunta.

I had been ninth in seniority on the Euclid City Council, but the death of Ed Sustarsic suddenly moved me up to the number eight position. City Council President Kosmetos had for years adhered to the concept that City Council chairmanships were to be dispersed based on seniority alone. That's the reason why being ninth on the depth chart left me without a chairmanship on a council that had only eight committees.

I looked forward to controlling the agenda at meetings of the somewhat obscure committee. The Coalition had other ideas.

Kosmetos announced that he would ask the Coalition council to break with tradition and his previously stated policy. Legislation was introduced to give Jerry Sustarsic the committee chairmanship that I had been looking forward to.

Initially, Bill Demora, the Ward One Councilman who had loyally served the Coalition for years, griped that it didn't make sense to disregard City Council's long-standing seniority system. Chukayne had a little talk with Demora and at the very next meeting, Demora voted as he was directed. They gave the post to Jerry Sustarsic.

I was perturbed.

So perturbed that this little maneuver just increased my motivation. I felt re-energized in my campaign because the Coalition was doing everything it could to diminish me personally.

Some folks thought that the Coalition's action grew out of the Council President's anger over my attempt in 1986 to pass a resolution opposing the opening of the Perry nuclear plant several miles east of Euclid. Kosmetos worked for the massive electricity-producing corporation that operated the nuclear plant and it would have been embarrassing for him if my resolution had passed.

Although the obvious conflict of interest prevented Kosmetos from casting a vote, the remaining Coalition council members defeated my anti-nuclear resolution. But I don't think I lost out on that committee chairmanship because of the attitude that Kosmetos had toward me. I think it was just another example of typical Coalition arrogance.

Anatomy of a Political Power Play

Popular Coalition Councilman Ed Sustarsic dies, leaving a vacancy in the waste water committee chairmanship.

Council President Mike Kosmetos overrides my seniority, announcing plans to award the chair to Ed Sustarsic's nephew, Jerry Sustarsic.

Councilman Bill DeMora breaks rank from his Coalition cohorts and objects to the Sustarsic appointment, citing longstanding seniority rules.

Jerry Sustarsic is appointed Committee Chairman after Chukayne takes DeMora to the woodshed and brings him back into the fold.

And that's what made the Coalition's handling of this controversy so stupid. No one would have noticed if the City Council had quietly followed its own rules to make me head of the wastewater treatment committee. By denying me the opportunity, they called attention to their own expression of raw political power.

The *Euclid News Journal*, normally somewhat passive in the face of Fat Tony's machinations, even wrote an editorial criticizing the Coalition's attempt to marginalize me.

Citizens were beginning to talk about me more and more as a result. In the final analysis, they should've paid attention to Councilman Demora. At a time when the Coalition wanted to minimize my profile, they had increased it. They had inadvertently handed me another campaign issue and had generated public sympathy in my ongoing opposition to the great and powerful.

Joe Farrell thought this was a terrific development. He told me that the public loves a hopeful idealistic underdog.

I was just angry. But Joe had a good point.

Would the citizens remember the underdog in November?

CHAPTER SIXTEEN

Knock Knock

THIS CHAPTER could be a book all by itself. It traces my efforts in doing the one thing that Tony was never going to do.

Knock on doors.

No campaign literature, no matter how beautifully designed and printed, can compete with personal contact. Even if you could receive a mailer every day for a year, it couldn't compare with just one personal visit to your home. And phone calls can't compete with ringing the doorbell at your personal residence.

But if that was my strategy, that meant standing in the doorway of 17,000 homes.

17,000!

In Rocky IV, Sylvester Stallone looks up at his massive opponent from the Soviet Union and can't believe that he is about to face opposition poised to destroy anything in his path.

I faced a similarly daunting challenge.

I needed a bigger block of time. I had nine months.

270 days.

270 days in which to personally knock on those 17,000 doors.

Do the math. This would mean I would need to visit 63 homes per day for 270 days. Unbelievable as this sounds, that's exactly what I set out to do beginning in February 1987.

Timing was crucial. If I spent five minutes at each home that meant a little over five hours each day doing nothing but going up and down front walks of neighborhoods. How could I do that and run my private law practice at a pace that kept the bills paid?

Regardless, I had to disappear for several hours every day to do my impression of the Fuller Brush salesman.

And so I began.

And I learned more about people and about myself than I ever imagined.

First of all, I learned that people are not at home. They are at work, shopping, or doing whatever but most of the time they are not home. At any given moment, only about 25% of Euclid residents are at home. But that empty home could still get a handwritten note from me.

Dear Mrs. Smith, I personally came to your home today. I'm sorry I missed you. If you have any questions or comments that you'd like to call to my attention I would be interested in hearing from you so please feel free to call me at the number listed on the bottom of this card. I hope you'll consider voting for me in the upcoming mayor's race. Sincerely, Dave Lynch.

Many a resident told me that they were impressed with the handwritten note because it showed that the candidate himself was at their house.

Even if their busy lives took them away during my visit.

Each day the hours added up and I realized that I was up against a significant physical challenge. I was dressed in a suit, tie, and business shoes so that I could make a good impression on these residents. Unfortunately, business shoes are not the most comfortable way to engage in the amount of walking required to knock on 17,000 different doors.

I developed a real appreciation for mail carriers as I realized they too were wearing out shoe leather as part of their job every day.

Some of the lessons I learned came during the first few weeks of this door-to-door campaign. By the time the summer rolled around I knew how to efficiently accomplish this task. I learned that I had to keep moving. I had to resist the rookie mistakes I made during the first few days when I did things like spending valuable time arguing with someone who was a very strong Tony Giunta supporter.

I was merely allowing the enemy to take me off course by spending time with those that were never going to vote for me anyhow. Being the idealist, I actually saw value in trying to turn these people around during the initial days of this neighborhood canvassing. However, I learned that it was more important for me to make sure that I maintained my pace of walking throughout the neighborhoods so that every single home that housed a voter would experience this personal contact from me.

Another important lesson was skipping over homes where I was confident I was going to receive the votes anyhow. It was just as much a waste of time to exchange words of support with those that were in my corner to begin with.

Occasionally, I would bump into one of my supporters who knew I was in the neighborhood and wanted to know why I had passed them by. I explained the logic of using my face time on those that needed to be convinced.

To maintain speed, I also skipped over the homes where the board of elections printout showed no registered voter. These days, I would probably stop at these homes because the new laws would permit me to register the voters right there on the spot using forms that I could keep in my pocket. However, back then, too much time would have been wasted interacting with persons that were not likely to be voting on election day.

The door-knocking was the kind of thing where I could make a personal connection even if I stood on the doorstep for just a few seconds. For a nominal price, the Board of Elections provided all candidates a printout of the names of all the registered voters organized according to street address.

That meant that all I had to do was take the booklet and go up and down the street saying hello to each voter, greeting them by name.

Again, 75% of the residents were not home when I got there, but the printouts provided by the board of elections allowed me to personalize my handwritten note provided for the homeowner to find when they eventually got back home.

Of course, I picked up a lot of practical information along the way that allowed me to become a very efficient door-knocking machine by the time I hit my stride halfway through the campaign.

For example, I learned that most Euclid residents rarely use their front door and prefer to go in and out through a side door that opens out onto the driveway. Campaign literature left at the front of the house would frequently be ignored, left to yellow and fade and blow away into the bushes in the front yard.

I also learned that campaign literature needs to be firmly placed in a location where it will be found by the homeowner when they arrive home.

The simplest way to do this would be to open up the screen door at the side of the house and place the literature partly inside the door. You then close the screen door with the literature wedged in between the post of the doorway and the edge of the screen door.

Unfortunately, I would occasionally run into screen doors that were locked. I noticed that others leaving material for homeowners, such as vinyl siding companies or pizza delivery shops, would roll the literature into kind of a tube shape. They would wedge the tube shaped literature between the door handle and the screen door itself.

I saw that it would only take a few minutes for the winds blowing off Lake Erie to deposit this literature onto the ground, never to be seen by the homeowner. Where the homeowner had a locked screen door, I was forced to use some creativity and find a spot where the homeowner was sure to find my literature and my personal handwritten note.

Sometimes, I would stick the literature in the milk chute. Fortunately, Euclid is an older community and almost all the homes were built at a time when it was customary for the milkman to come by to leave dairy products.

Here I must make somewhat of a confession. There were those very rare instances when there was absolutely no way to leave my flyer in a place that could be found by Mr. and Mrs. Citizen. In those instances, I would resort to using the mailbox.

I've never received official confirmation of this, but I've always been told that it is a violation of federal law to use a residential mailbox for anything other than the United States mail. I've also heard that the mailman is instructed to throw the campaign literature away if he encounters election materials in a residential mailbox.

Fortunately, I didn't have to do this very often but it seems that some homes are virtually impervious to the deposit of campaign information when the homeowner is not home. Especially challenging were homes that had stickers attached to the screen doors with the words "no soliciting" emblazoned across them. I did some research on this matter and realized that there are various state laws that permit homeowners to ban door-to- door salesmen.

I also learned that campaigning politicians are exempt from these laws because the First Amendment protects political speech. Nonetheless, I would occasionally run into a homeowner who insisted that I read the sticker and obey it. I would usually leave that home without even identifying myself. This homeowner was already mad at me just for showing up.

There were lots of other tricks to be learned along the way.

One of the biggest areas important for the door-to-door politician involves dogs. Lots of Euclid residents have dogs that would begin barking long before I even got close to the doorbell. I used to be afraid of dogs when I was kid but I grew out of that fear as I got older.

Now I was trying to communicate with people in their homes and dogs of all sizes presented a challenge. That's why I was so happy that Joe Farrell taught me the importance of the screen door footstop (also known as the "Joe Farrell footstop").

Many times I would approach a home and the main door was wide open with the screen door closed but not latched. This would mean there was danger of being bitten because a large dog would come crashing against the unlatched screen door, pushing it open and coming outside to bite my ankle before the homeowner could get up off the couch to see who was there.

Joe Farrell instructed me to keep my foot pushed against the bottom of the screen door so that Fido could be kept indoors until his owner appeared. This was a great technique that saved my hide on many occasions.

Joe told me that one time a large German Shepherd had to go to the hospital with terrible wounds from broken glass because Joe put his foot against the bottom of the screen door while Cujo crashed against the glass in the screen door, breaking the glass, canine blood all over the place.

Another thing I had to watch out for was the family that was too welcoming. Part of the success of this process of visiting people on a door-to-door basis meant that you really had to keep moving. Remember the calculation I made showed that I could not spend more than five minutes at each household.

This was pretty easy to keep up with because so many people were not home. However, occasionally a family would invite me to sit down and that's when I knew I was in trouble. You appreciate the hospitality but you have to keep moving.

Sometimes sitting down would be followed by an offer of something to eat or drink. I could tell that some folks would be offended if I refused this hospitality. I've had some pretty strange foods as a result but for the most part it was a positive experience.

Perhaps the most interesting part of campaigning door-to-door is the fact that the resident was frequently very surprised to see me. Everybody is used to seeing Jehovah's Witnesses or Boy Scouts or even some kind of special interest group trying to gather petition signatures. However, nobody expects to see a candidate in person asking for your vote.

As long as there was some daylight, I would continue knocking. On those long summer days that would mean stopping by someone's house as late as eight o'clock at night. I didn't care. As long as it was warm and the sun was out, I kept going. I was driven.

One of the most memorable experiences involved a naked lady. One hot Sunday afternoon in August I came to a home where the front door was wide open so I had to knock on the screen door. The sun was low in the sky and I can remember that the doorbell was broken.

Now some of the screen doors are made out of a soft plastic and you really have to rap hard with your knuckles to make enough noise to get someone's attention inside the house. I knocked very loudly and then peered in through the screen.

On the La-Z-Boy recliner right in the front living room I could make out the figure of a beautiful brunette with very long hair and porcelain skin. She must have wanted to cool off because she was lying down on the lounge chair with a fan blowing on her.

My banging on the door so startled her that she leaned onto her side and fell right off the chair. I guess she had been sleeping. She hit the floor with a crash and then sprang to her feet, not coming to the door, but instead darting across the room.

It was then that I noticed that this young lady was racing from her fall to another room so that she could put some clothes on. She was completely naked. I began to tip-toe down the steps of her porch to move on to the next house.

However, before I could do so she re-emerged at the door wearing a robe, assuming that I had not seen a thing. Of course, I acted like I hadn't seen anything and gave her my normal political pitch along with a piece of literature.

As I went up the walkway to the next house I started thinking about the way she had been looking at me while we were speaking. I could see in her eyes that she was wondering if I had actually observed her birthday suit. I wore a poker face throughout that conversation but I remember telling my wife when I got home that there was an important lesson to be learned.

No matter how hot it is, close the front door before you lounge around naked in the living room.

I also learned not to get too excited when I received an exuberant response from citizens. In one house a man came to the door and after asking me a few questions told me that he was very impressed by my enthusiasm and by my plans to improve government in Euclid. He shook my hand and told me that I could count on him on election day.

Unfortunately, my hearing is too good. As I was walking away from the door I could hear the man tell his wife "that's the son of a bitch that's running against Tony!"

Generally speaking, I was making a positive impression throughout the community and I was doing it in a way that was virtually invisible: quiet and very gradual in its pace.

There's no doubt that this was a case of the tortoise and the hare. I was the steady-paced turtle while Tony was the hare.

Even though I talked about a number of issues, I began to realize that what I really needed to do was leave people with a positive impression of me that they would remember when they went to the polls. I wish I had a dollar for each time that someone said they would vote for me because I "seemed like a nice young man."

I saw that this was the best strategy in campaigning on front stoops. The average citizen wasn't looking for burning issues when

I met them on their doorstep. What they wanted was someone who would be willing to look them in the eye and speak with conviction.

My youth, which was a disadvantage when I started, really seemed to be in my favor. Essentially, by meeting me in person, citizens in Euclid began to feel good about the idea that a youthful professional with a young bride and a couple of kids was running for mayor.

For senior citizens, my candidacy told them that Euclid was a place with a good future where young families like mine could make a difference. The younger voters related to me as one of their own. They sensed that I represented the chance to affect a change from the stodgy, good-old-boy network to progressive thinking with modern ideas.

Every direct contact with the citizen in this doorbell campaign concluded with my giving a firm handshake and a promise to justify their faith in me if they should put me in office. The days grew long and I became weary as I approached completing this marathon sometime toward the end of the second week in October. I can remember how I was filled with doubt.

Had I wasted hundreds of hours when I should've been toiling away at my law practice to support my family? What would become of me if I lost this race and became another statistic, another losing candidate chewed up by the Coalition?

Nancy and I had a lot of heart-to-heart talks many evenings when I staggered home in the dark with sore feet–cold and dejected.

What would the future hold for us?

CHAPTER SEVENTEEN

The Giuntadome

THE EXPENSE OF CITY GOVERNMENT soared in the mid-to-late 1980s. This is when healthcare costs began to take off, decimating the city budget that provided medical insurance to all full-time employees and their families. Salt for the roads, utilities, and virtually everything else was skyrocketing in cost as well.

To make matters worse, the local economy was hurting. Since a local payroll tax was the main source of municipal revenue, a slow local economy meant less cash in city coffers.

Perhaps the biggest blow ever dealt to the Euclid economy took place under Mayor Giunta's watch. Just a couple of years prior to the election, Euclid's biggest employer, TRW, announced it was leaving town. The impact on city tax revenue was significant. What made it even more painful was the fact that TRW had moved its entire operation to another suburban city just a ten-minute drive away.

Tony, however, was made of teflon. The public didn't blame him for TRW's departure.

I floated the following theory: Tony should've been in touch with TRW leadership before the move was even contemplated. He was so disconnected from the TRW management team that he never had a chance to head them off at the pass to change their mind. In other words, Tony was so out of touch that this crippling event occurred in the Euclid economy and Tony didn't even know it was coming.

Unfortunately for me, the community was angry at TRW, not Tony. The citizens just didn't buy my idea that Tony could've done more to save TRW.

Of course, all Northeast Ohio was struggling during this period. Given the economy, Euclid's job losses weren't entirely Tony's fault and it seems most folks were willing to give Tony the benefit of the doubt. Blue-collar Euclid loved blue-collar Tony. However, Tony and the Coalition continued to spend, taking risks with the city budget. A slow economy meant fewer jobs and reduced tax collections. Despite this, the Mayor and the Coalition forged ahead with Tony's pet project, building a new City Hall.

And this wasn't just a new City Hall. It was a new municipal complex, complete with a new Municipal Court building and a new city jail. The space for the administration was going to be ten times the size of the old building that had been used since 1937.

Tony had a point. The old City Hall was functional but modern city government had outgrown it and not just because Tony couldn't control his hiring of political hacks.

Special programs for senior citizens, economic development, and the administration of federal funds weren't even contemplated when the old building was constructed in the late 1930's. Combine this with the fact that the city government was now serving a population almost five times the size it was back then, and you couldn't disagree the new building was needed.

But with all of Euclid struggling, Tony's timing was wrong-headed.

And I knew that this new building under construction in the middle of the campaign could be an important issue.

The construction site was huge, right in the middle of town where virtually every voter drove by every day. Fat Tony had a gigantic sign placed upfront facing East 222nd Street so everyone could read who was responsible. You've seen the type of sign I'm referring to.

Stark black lettering on the massive white board proclaimed that Tony Giunta, assisted by his cabinet, was the moving force behind the monstrosity that was slowly taking shape.

The centerpiece of the new complex was the City Council chamber. It was an enormous round room with a ceiling 65 feet high.

It had a tiered, theater-style gallery for citizens to observe the proceedings and an elevated stage where Tony anticipated he would preside in an edifice finally up to the style he deserved. The design really was magnificent with its white marble walls. The new Council chamber was the Roman forum outfitted with modern technology. It looked very expensive.

And it was. Perhaps the most prominent feature of the council chambers was the domed ceiling. The dome was quite conspicuous and could be seen from blocks away.

If you've ever been to Washington, D.C., you know how instantly recognizable the dome of the Capitol is. That huge white dome rising on Euclid's main drag was the trademark feature of the new complex.

For this reason, Tony illuminated the construction site so the glory of the Coalition could shine for all to see at night. Even though the new building wasn't scheduled for completion until well after the election, Tony wanted to remind voters of his stature throughout the campaign. Tony and his cronies saw the new project as the ultimate symbol of his power and achievement.

But it was symbolic of other things as well.

Symbolic of reckless overspending at a time when city government needed to pull back. The dark clouds of economic storms were threatening families in our city and Tony and the Coalition were building something big and expensive.

It's funny how people associate the person with a project or concept. Think Obamacare or Reaganomics.

Well, a disgruntled policeman came up with a name for the Mayor's crowning project. I can't take credit for it but I knew I'd be able to use it. The new Council chamber was dubbed the "Giuntadome". The name stuck.

In fact, it went what would be considered viral for 1987.

I'd been handed a big issue.

The Giuntadome became a battle cry for my campaign.

The Giuntadome in all it's glory.

The Giuntadome's council chamber interior: magnificent but pricey.

Late one night with the election only three days away, a local celebrity, Chuck Booms, went out with a couple of friends and taped a huge paper banner to the front of the construction fence that surrounded the still incomplete Giuntadome.

Tony's illuminated sign read "Your tax dollars at work".

Chuck Booms' banner read "Your tax dollars at waste".

The Giuntadome.

That one word crystallized my criticism of a corrupt, overspending government out of touch with the needs of the people.

Amazingly, the one issue I pressed forward most in my campaign was the very thing that Giunta himself was promoting as a sign of his leadership. If Giunta was right I was reminding voters of one of Tony's greatest achievements. If I were right, Giunta was highlighting the most visible example of his incompetence.

Who was right?

I bet the house on the Giuntadome issue.

On election day the voters would call my bet.

I prayed for aces.

CHAPTER EIGHTEEN

Jochum

MARK JOCHUM. He's part of this story as well.

Jochum was a member of the Loyal Opposition, along with Joe Farrell and myself. Mark and Joe had a rough time of it as the voices in the wilderness.

Mark also had a lot to live down. You see, Mark was nicknamed "The Spoiler". He had an interesting history.

The first Coalition Mayor after Ken Sims was a Republican named Harry Knuth. Knuth was a throwback to the old Coalition, having been elected to City Council in 1937 as part of the Ken Sims slate that restored integrity to City Hall. He took a shine to Jochum, an idealistic young insurance agent. Knuth encouraged him to get involved in city politics and Jochum became Knuth's protegé.

After Sims retired, Knuth finished out his remaining term of office and then was elected mayor in his own right. After only one term, at Rocco's insistence, Knuth surprised everyone in Euclid by announcing that he would not run again. Rocco was in charge now and the ways of Ken Sims were being replaced by the Law Director's vision.

Jochum resented the shabby way Rocco treated his mentor. Jochum swore to get his revenge by opposing the Coalition from that time on. They dumped his hero so he was going to dump them. A few years later, Jochum was elected the Ward Two councilman and he made a point of expressing his disgust with the Coalition.

Just when it seemed Joe Farrell was poised to end the Coalition's vise-like grip on local government in 1979, Mark Jochum jumped into the mayor's race as a last-minute third candidate.

Truth be told, if Jochum hadn't entered that race, Joe Farrell would have become the mayor that year. For this reason, there developed a tension between Mark and Joe. Joe had to move forward with his career in politics as the vocal minority, but to his chagrin, his only ally until I came along was Mark Jochum.

There were those in town who thought Mark was somewhat of a sinister force. These observers saw Mark Jochum as actually working behind enemy lines for the Coalition.

A plant.

A weasel.

After all, he had been close to former Coalition Mayor Harry Knuth. And despite the Coalition's claims that Jochum was an integrationist, much of Jochum's rhetoric on the council floor opposed Federal assistance programs because he didn't like the strings attached to Federal money.

Jochum and his mentor, Mayor Knuth: Jochum never forgave Rocco for the way Knuth was treated. Have you ever seen so much plaid and stripes at one time?

Was Jochum in reality a Benedict Arnold? What other explanation could there be for ruining Joe Farrell's chance to free our city from the clutches of the Evil Empire?

And it was oh so evil.

On top of that, Jochum didn't always behave as if he were really willing to hold Fat Tony's feet to the fire. Joe Farrell was always introducing legislation designed to force the Coalition to be more accountable for its actions. Oddly, Jochum frequently opposed Joe's efforts.

Few could explain it. This, however, just exacerbated the thinly veiled distrust between the Farrell and Jochum camps.

As my campaign rolled forward, I had to count on people I could lean on.

Joe was always there.

At events.

At campaign meetings.

An ear open for late-night consultation and well, moral support.

In contrast, Jochum remained aloof. He did nothing to help. It's almost as if he said, "Good luck, kid. I hope you win, but you're on your own."

Mark would occasionally catch me after a Council meeting to see how things were going. I didn't reveal much. There were too many questions surrounding his true allegiance. A few folks told me not to worry about Mark too much. Their theory was that Mark still harbored visions of his own unfulfilled glory. The possibility that Lynch might grab the brass ring Mark had earned himself seemed to grate on Mr. Jochum.

We held our breath all the way through the deadline for filing petitions for the mayor's race in August of 1987. We half expected that Mark Jochum would repeat his vote-splitting performance and jump into the race at the last second. We were relieved when the filing deadline line passed and Jochum remained a non-candidate.

Despite this, we were wary of him. Joe remained my reliable friend on City Council, and most importantly, my faithful advisor.

From a distance, we kept an eye on Jochum.

And then we forged ahead.

CHAPTER NINETEEN

Fixed Count

THE COALITION'S SUPERB RECORD of electoral victories wasn't hurt by the practice of polling place vote counting.

Polling place vote counting was a long-standing practice that simplified the work of the centralized Cuyahoga County Board of Elections.

While the county board in downtown Cleveland was required to certify municipal election results because of state law, polling place vote counting saved the board time and money.

Here's how it worked.

Each voting location was manned by poll workers who were charged with keeping the voting activity efficient and fair. At the end of the night, the polls would close.

With centralized counting downtown, the ballots would be secured, bundled, and transported to the Board of Elections headquarters for counting and certification of results. Unfortunately, this was not the practice back then.

Instead, the Board of Elections allowed the presiding judge and three assistants to open the voting machines and count the votes right there on site where the votes were cast. The presiding judge and the three assistants carefully reconfirmed the count and then sent the bundled ballots downtown with a note attached reflecting the results. The county board then just accepted the count contained in the report from the local polling place.

Essentially, the board relied on the presiding judge and these three assistants to do the counting for them: polling place vote counting. The presiding judge would also hand-write the results for that polling place on a piece of paper and tape the results to the door of the building.

You could figure out the results of a local election by driving from one voting location to another, taking down the results taped to the door, and doing the math. It was easy.

The system kept things honest by requiring that the polling place officials were half-Republican and half-Democrat, appointed by the local party organization in each municipality. This is where the Coalition showed its ingenious design.

Since the Coalition consisted of both Republicans and Democrats, the Coalition itself controlled the local parties through its own operatives. The president of the Euclid Republican party was a Coalitionist. The president of the Euclid Democratic party was a Coalitionist.

This meant that the people doing the counting at the local polling place were 100% Coalition members. Frank Chukayne hand-picked the presiding judges and their assistants who counted the vote at the end of the night. It's no wonder that every mayor's race was won by the Coalition candidate for 50 years running. It was depressing to think that my campaign would culminate in a vote-count conducted by the enemy.

It was like playing the New York Yankees using umpires paid by the Steinbrenner family.

We plowed ahead anyway. After all, lying about the vote-totals was a crime.

We prayed for integrity from these sweet retired ladies that were pegged for the jobs at the polling places. They seemed to take their responsibilities very seriously.

Would they let the kid get a true count?

Against the Coalition?

We could only wait and see.

CHAPTER TWENTY

Mafia

ONE DAY while canvassing the neighborhood for votes, I noticed a dark blue Chevrolet Impala parked up the street about ten houses beyond where I was knocking on doors.

I paid no attention to it until the next day. I noticed the same car parked down the street from me as I knocked on doors in a completely different neighborhood about a mile away from where I had been the day before. When the same car appeared the third day I was spooked.

All the windows and windshields had a dark tint so if someone was in the car, I couldn't tell.

And it was just…there.

I never noticed it arriving or leaving at any time. I had this feeling that someone inside that blue Chevy Impala was watching me. I was a little frightened.

This required a session with Joe Farrell, the one man who knew the Coalition like no other and who knew what I was going through. I called Joe after the sun went down. He told me to stop by his house at 9 PM.

It was a Monday night. I was ushered into the familiar kitchen where Joe had offered his counsel to me so many times before. Joe listened quietly to the tale of the sedan watching me from a distance. I finished.

Joe looked at me, got up to take a six-pack of beer from the pantry, and tossed it into the pullout freezer that constituted the bottom third of his Frigidaire. The look on his face told me it was going to be a long night.

Joe then began to recount the evidence of the Coalition's ties to the mob.

The Mafia.

His tone was quiet as he spoke of violent men who sold protection.

The scene at the Farrell household was surreal. It reminded me of one my favorite moments in the movie "Jaws".

Quint, the grizzled shark hunter, sits in the galley, Roy Scheider and Richard Dreyfuss listening with rapt attention. The old salt describes the terrifying scene of sailors stranded in the ocean waiting for rescue.

The sharks circle, bump them, and then eat them alive, survivors unable to forget the fear that stays with them for the rest of their lives.

Here are the highlights of Joe's revelations.

It seems that Fat Tony and Pat Rocco liked to hang out with Anthony Liberatore. Joe knew this because Fat Tony introduced Joe to Tony Liberatore in a Euclid bar one night.

Fat Tony put his arm around Liberatore and described him as "my dear friend". Liberatore was well known as the head of the Cleveland branch of La Cosa Nostra during a particularly bloody period in the late 1970s.

Anthony Liberatore was on the FBI's Most wanted list until his apprehension for the Danny Green murder.

Mafia hits made headlines about every three months in those days. It culminated in 1982 when Liberatore was convicted for his involvement in the bombing death of Danny Green. This infamous mob execution made it clear that Tony Liberatore had no problem protecting Mafia turf through the use of terror.

The recent Hollywood film "Kill The Irishman" portrays the drama that unfolded in Northeast Ohio when Danny Green paid the ultimate price for taking over the crooked Longshoremen's union. The Mob didn't like it when someone outmobbed them. Liberatore ordered the elimination of Green.

Danny Green got into his Cadillac outside a medical building in Lyndhurst, a fashionable suburb just south of Euclid. Several attempts to place a bomb in the engine compartment had failed so Liberatore solved the problem by having the explosives placed in a car parked next to Green's shiny blue El Dorado. The blast was so intense parts of Danny Green were never recovered.

Danny Green pushed the mob too far. He knew his days were numbered.

And according to Joe, the Coalition cronies were Liberatore's pals. Joe's voice was almost at a whisper now. My mind was racing. What did this mean?

Clearly, my adversaries had very scary friends.

Joe then talked about one of Rocco's staff attorneys who told Joe about an encounter with one of these Coalition "associates" from the underworld. Dave Lombardo was a brilliant lawyer recruited by the Law Director to join the city's stable of legal eagles. Before Lombardo could be placed on the payroll, he had to be interviewed by a "businessman" from Youngstown. Youngstown, Ohio was the steel town generally acknowledged as the capital city for the mafia in the Midwest.

A steady stream of federal indictments came out of Youngstown after an extensive FBI investigation culminated in the conviction of Youngstown's gadfly congressman. U.S. Representative James Trafficant went to Club Fed for acts of bribery and racketeering.

Youngstown was to organized crime in 1987 what Silicon Valley is to computer technology today. Lombardo went to see the unnamed power broker at a Youngstown address supplied by Rocco. Lombardo received the required blessing but was somewhat baffled by the experience. Lombardo wondered if he had just spent a few moments in the presence of the Godfather himself. He would never know for certain the exacty identity of the gentleman but he assured Joe that the fellow was not a savory character.

And then there was the Joe Cali incident.

Joe Farrell left the kitchen table for a moment to retrieve an ice-cold Coors from the freezer. He grabbed the beer but made a detour to a bookshelf in the sun room before returning to the kitchen.

From the top shelf, he pulled out an old legal-size manila envelope. He sat down next to me and unclasping the flap of the envelope, he pulled out a newspaper clipping.

It showed a photograph of Euclid police detectives walking among debris in front of a house that appeared to have been blown up. The caption read "HOME BLASTED-detectives look at the rubble left in the wake of a mysterious explosion at 1 AM today at the home of Euclid contractor Joseph Cali."

Farrell gave the details.

It seems that Mr. Cali borrowed a sizable sum from the local Brotherhood Loan Company. Cali had welched on repayment. Crime bosses don't like that sort of thing.

So they asked Eugene Ciasullo to send a message to Mr. Cali. Ciasullo was nicknamed "The Animal" because of his callous disregard for human life.

Eugene "The Animal" blew up Joe Cali's house in Euclid.

What's that got to do with the Coalition?

That's the thing, Joe said.

The police never arrested a suspect.

In fact, Cali moved to Florida shortly after the bombing, never pressing the police for an arrest.

So why didn't Chief Payne go after "The Animal"? According to Joe, The Animal bragged about his exploits. Everyone at City Hall knew the identity of the bomber.

Everyone, it appears, except for the Coalition controlled Police Department. According to Joe, Fat Tony and Pat Rocco knew better than to get in the way of their Mafia friends.

And it was common knowledge that Chief Payne frequented The Theatrical, a favorite downtown hangout for organized crime figures.

It all seemed to fit.

Contractors bribing Coalition leadership to obtain lucrative contracts.

Mafia kingpins cozying up to city officials.

Elections rigged by controlling the vote count before the ballots went to the county elections board for tabulation.

Prospective City lawyers traveling to Youngstown to kiss somebody's ring.

Homes bombed without investigation.

I'd always had suspicions. Rumors about such things abounded.

Now Joe confirmed my fears.

Police review the rubble after the Cali bombing.

SUPPLEMENTARY REPORT

OFFENSE Departmental Information   DATE OF OFFENSE Feb. 13, 19 73   TIME 1:08 A.M.

COMPLAINANT Joseph Cali   RESIDENCE 26441 Briardale Ave.,

PLACE OF OCCURENCE 26441 Briardale Ave.

REPORT BY John D. Zak   RANK Sgt.   DATE Feb. 13, 19 73

EXAMINED AND APPROVED BY [signature]   RANK Lt,   DATE Feb. 13, 19 73

Lt. Grze Sir:

On this date at 1:08 AM there was a report of a loud explosion, that was heard in all parts of the City. A report was received that the explosion was at 26441 Briardale Ave.,

Upon my arrival at the scene, parts of the siding from the home had been blown across the street. The front picture window of the house had been blown into the living room, under the front window, and approx. 3 foot from the front steps was a hole in the foundation, also a hole in the ground approx. 18 inches deep, about 4 foot across. The block was blown into the basement. A heavy odor of burnt powder was present. The slab and the side of the steps were broken. The block in the basement was blown across the recreation rm. This section of wall was approx. 4 foot wide, and 6 foot high.

The home is owned by a Joseph Cali, white male, who is in the construction business. He claims that he has no trouble with the unions, or business associates, and has no problems with his workers. He stated that he and his wife Sarah went to bed at approx. 12 or 12:30 AM, his daughter, Debbie had gone to bed earlier, when they were awakened by a loud explosion. He got out of bed and went into the living room and found the front window glass, and frame inside the house. He then went outside and saw the hole in his basement wall. Photographs were taken by Ptl. Steinmetz, Captl Willcocks arrived on the scene, and took over the investigation.

At this time 8 other homes were damaged by the concusion. Various windows being broken. Firemen reported as they were going South on E. 260 St., a green van was North-bound, and that the driver seemed to watch the truck. They related that when they arrived on Briardale that the same truck stopped on E. 266 St., and Briardale and seemed to watch the action. Later I talked to Dan McPeek who lives a few doors from the above location, and he stated that the concusion from the bomb knocked his lamp over and that he was struck in the head by same, he got out of bed and looked out the door, and as he did so he saw a green van truck going down the street at a high rate of speed.

Men have been assigned to guard the home until a daylight investigation can be made.

Respectfully submitted,

John D. Zak Sgt

THIS FORM TO BE USED TO REPORT INVESTIGATIONS, ADDITIONAL INFORMATION ON CRIMES REPORTED, MISSING PERSONS LOCATED OR OFFENSES, STATEMENTS OF WITNESSES, CASES CLEARED AND CLOSED.

Report on the bombing: no suspects.

I was scared. Joe could tell. But then he told me two things would probably protect me from harm.

First, the mob rarely caused harm to candidates already publicly declared. It would be too obvious. It would also be too easy for the FBI to connect the dots between Fat Tony and my demise.

Secondly, Joe said, I wasn't really a threat to the Coalition. They weren't afraid of me because I had no chance, given the choke hold they had on local politics.

Nope, said Joe, I was in no danger. They just want to keep an eye on me, he said.

So don't worry about it. Just keep on doing what I was doing and enjoy the ride. When I see the Impala, Joe suggested, just smile and give a little wave.

Don't worry?

I was worried.

CHAPTER TWENTY-ONE

Oyaski

AN INTERESTING FEATURE of the all-powerful Coalition was that it also attracted good people. After all, if you wanted to work in local government, the only viable path in Euclid led to the Coalition party.

Within their midst, the Coalition had someone that, if cultivated properly, could have helped the Coalition party for many years to come.

His name was Paul Oyaski.

Just a couple of years older than myself, Oyaski was a sharp-witted attorney recruited by the Coalition to run for the Ward 3 Council seat prior to George Carson assuming that position.

Oyaski was young, articulate, and dynamic. Truth is, he could have been a threat to the Coalition as well.

But these guys were smart. Oyaski first came to the attention of the Coalition's top brass when Oyaski was a teenager hired for a summer job in the city's service department. Paul stood out from the crowd of kids brought on board to cut grass and pick up trash.

He was an energetic worker but what really distinguished him was his native intelligence and easy way with people. The other kids just naturally gravitated to him. He was what some might describe as a natural born leader.

Oyaski went on to college and then law school but the city's service director remembered the bright young man who had made such a positive impression. Oyaski's law degree made him a must-have commodity for the Coalition hungry for some new blood to carry on the legacy.

They recruited Oyaski and he couldn't resist. He was flattered to be asked into the Coalition circle and his subsequent City Council victory as the Coalition's Ward 3 candidate in 1977 solidified the relationship.

Although he was re-elected to his council seat in 1979, Oyaski was so impressive that he never finished his second term. The directors were the Mayor's cabinet and the Mayor needed to fill a vacancy in the fairly new position of Development Director.

As the era of federal grants emerged, Rocco thought it would be a good idea to designate Oyaski at the tender age of 29 for the new post. It was brilliant.

Oyaski immersed himself in the new federal guidelines and became a self-taught expert in the field. More importantly, Oyaski now worked directly for Fat Tony. Oyaski became one of the boys. Rocco felt Oyaski could be controlled.

Giunta gives Oyaski the oath of office as a new councilman.

That's what gave me pause. Oyaski and I shared a desire to make government work for the people. But he had gone over to the dark side. You'd have to be blind not to see all the corruption taking place within the Coalition administration.

There was scuttlebutt that Oyaski was particularly disgusted when he discovered a sidewalk inspector on the city payroll who never showed up for work. The inspector brazenly went to work in a local retail shop while he was supposed to be on duty as a city employee. The taxpayers funded this fraud.

Although Oyaski despised this sort of activity, he was still willing to be part of the Coalition infrastructure.

I liked the idea that somebody was on the inside complaining about the ethical practices of Fat Tony's administration.

Even more encouraging was Oyaski's conspicuous absence from a newspaper photo showing the whole Coalition gang breaking ground for the new City Hall construction. Maybe word of Oyaski's opposition to the new building was more than just a rumor. We'd been told that Oyaski's internal squawking about the Giuntadome had made him the target of Chukayne's ire.

Oyaski had been promised that because of his carping, his department would never see the inside of the new palace. Oyaski would be banished to the old City Hall building while those who obediently kept their mouths shut would enjoy the magnificent new edifice.

But it still bothered me that Oyaski was willing to remain part of this evil band. From a political standpoint, the Coalition seemed even more potent with this smart young lawyer on their team. He was the kind of person who could figure out ways to counter the campaign tactics that I employed.

It was Oyaski who told Rocco that the poll of July 1987 was ominous for Mayor Giunta because of the large number of undecided voters. Oyaski reasoned that an attractive opponent who captured the undecided voters only had to steal away a few of Tony's supporters to prevail.

Rocco found Oyaski's theory laughable. No challenger could bring all of the uncertain voters into his camp in the face of the campaign Rocco had designed.

With Oyaski's youthful energy and intellectual capability though, Fat Tony had a valuable asset and it made me realize that the mountain I was trying to climb was certainly Everest in proportion.

Was Oyaski willing to use his talents to guarantee another victory for the Coalition? We would soon see.

But even if Oyaski could develop some outstanding ideas to help push Tony over the top, another question would have to be answered first.

Was the Coalition smart enough to listen to Oyaski? Rocco had a pretty big ego and I was hoping that the Coalition just might think that they didn't have to listen to Oyaski. Fat Tony and Pat Rocco were quite confident in the outcome of this election.

Perhaps their overconfidence meant that Oyaski's input would be kept in the background. Better yet, Oyaski's occasional objections to various Coalition maneuvers, even if kept between Oyaski and the inner circle, might render him *persona non grata* in Rocco's eyes. Rocco tended to freeze out directors when he sniffed even a hint of disloyalty.

I half expected that Giunta's reelection might be followed by the firing of Oyaski. That's the way they did things. I guessed that Giunta and Rocco were not listening to Paul. If true, that would be a bonus for my campaign.

I could only hope.

CHAPTER TWENTY-TWO

The Brave Cop

RONALD STIH was a Euclid patrol officer who lived two doors away from my home on Mallard Avenue.

He couldn't stand Rocco and Giunta. Like most of the policemen, he resented the way their excesses led to shortchanging the police budget.

So Ron Stih did something no Euclid policeman had ever done. He openly supported a Coalition Mayor's opponent. He told the world he wanted Dave Lynch to win the race.

He did it in a way that was bound to attract attention and get him in trouble at work. He put a "Lynch for Mayor" sign on his front lawn. Then a few others wearing the blue uniform of the Euclid police department followed his lead and did the same.

Chief Payne was angry.

He assembled his lieutenants and captains to formulate a response. Chief Payne told his department heads that it wasn't about Stih's political choice.

According to Payne, it was wrong for policemen to become politically involved. A cop was always above politics, he said.

This was laughable. Chief Payne was up to his badge in Coalition politics. Fat Tony was constantly having the Chief fix a speeding ticket or tear up a parking citation.

It was somewhat embarrassing for the Chief when a determined outsider forced the re-opening of the murder case against Judge Robert Steele, a file closed by Payne's detectives without an arrest. Eight years after the murder, the former President of the Euclid Coalition Party was finally brought to justice because FBI agent Robert Ressler refused to abide Payne's desire to bury the whole matter.

Eyebrows were raised when the Chief compromised his department with the non-investigation of the bombing of the Joe Cali household by the local Mafioso.

All this evidence makes it clear that the Law Director and the Mayor had a willing ally in Frank Payne, the man who had been head of the police department longer than any other chief in the State of Ohio.

Chief Payne refused to come to the aid of one of his officers threatened with dismissal when the cop's only offense was issuing a well-deserved traffic ticket to Giunta's teenage son who had carelessly passed a school bus unloading children. The officer held on to his job but no thanks to Payne. Giunta and Rocco let the guy off the hook but it was clear that the officer's chances for promotion were nil.

Chukayne also saw to it that the police department was used as a source of patronage jobs. Civil service tests were required to become a policeman, but the Chief also employed dispatchers, office staff, and corrections officers. These were posts the Coalition could offer in return for political loyalty. What did the Chief get out of the arrangement?

The Coalition gave him total autonomy in running his department. He liked that. Play ball with the Coalition and they'll leave you alone to run your own turf.

Chief Payne was the king of local law enforcement. Frank Payne joined the police department the same year the Coalition was created in 1937. When I threw my hat into the ring to run against Fat Tony in 1987, Payne was in his fifty-first year in law enforcement.

His second floor office was decorated with photographs featuring the Chief with celebrities who wanted to rub elbows with the law enforcement legend. The Coalition loved Chief Payne because he gave them what they wanted and kept his mouth shut about it.

The icon: Chief Frank Payne

But they also loved him because he was the common thread from the old Ken Sims days of the Coalition in the 1930s. The Chief was a symbol of the staying power of Coalition politics. It had old roots and like a giant sequoia, it would be around forever.

He was like J. Edgar Hoover. Rumor had it that he had a secret file on everyone at City Hall, especially mouthy councilmen. He had immense power and he wasn't going anywhere.

He was an historical figure worshiped by the citizens. He could easily have become Mayor himself. But he didn't want that. He liked operating as the senior statesman of law enforcement in the state of Ohio.

No one questioned his edicts. His reputation was such that no one could touch him.

The situation was analogous to the big college campus where the President and Board of Trustees are the publicly identified leaders of the University. But the long tenured head football coach who wins games makes more money than the college president and his demands are always fulfilled.

Think Joe Paterno before the Jerry Sandusky scandal. Payne cited platitudes about the importance of political neutrality but he was just teed-off because one of his charges was wandering off the reservation.

This editorial cartoon captured Payne's power.

I can hear Fat Tony now, calling Chief Payne about it. Payne, I'm sure, told Tony not to worry. The Chief would handle Ron Stih and his cohorts.

So after the meeting with his brain trust, Payne asked Rocco for a legal opinion to deal with the mutinous Patrolman Stih.

Patrolman Ron Stih kept on smiling despite the Coalition's attempt to punish him for having an opinion.

Rocco delivered. The offending policemen were brought up on charges for violating the Hatch Act.

The Hatch Act is a federal law proclaiming that civil servants must refrain from political activity. Stih and company faced fines, suspension, and possible termination. High price to pay for planting a lawn sign.

They hired a private attorney, stunning the Chief and the Coalition. You were supposed to roll over. Didn't Stih know who he was dealing with? It's Chief Payne, the icon.

It should be noted here that Patrol Officer Ron Stih had some special motivation in standing up to the Coalition.

When I ran for the Ward 3 council seat in 1985, I published a piece of political literature that outlined my undying commitment to supporting the police department. The Coalition hated this because they knew they were vulnerable, given the police union's complaints about underfunding safety forces.

The literature featured a photograph of me talking to an unidentified Euclid police officer who had his back to the camera, no badge visible to identify the cop. The policeman's name was Jim Reed and his disgust with the Coalition was typical for the grunt on the beat in 1985. He didn't like the Chief's playing ball with the Coalition politicians and he detested the city's cheap funding policy for basic patrolmen.

Unfortunately, despite his back to the camera, Reed did not remain anonymous as intended in that photo shoot. You see, Jim Reed had a large birth mark on his left forearm and none of us thought about it when we posed that picture.

With that birthmark visible in the snapshot, Reed was easily identified when that literature was circulated in the 1985 Ward 3 Council campaign against George Carson. Reed was a marked man after that. No formal charges were brought against him but Payne's lieutenants made it clear that he had crossed a line that the Coalition wouldn't allow.

Jim Reed was one of Ron Stih's best friends on the force. That's why this next chilling event made Ron Stih pause. A few months after my Ward Three Council election, Jim Reed died under very suspicious circumstances.

Reed was an avid skydiver. As a police officer, he was used to paying meticulous attention to detail.

One afternoon, Jim Reed's parachute failed to open and he fell to his death somewhere over Canton, Ohio. There were lots of theories and plenty of speculation as to what actually happened.

But Ron Stih always carried Jim in his heart and an uncertain uneasiness in the back of his mind. Had the Coalition been somehow involved in the parachute disaster? I told Ron that even the Coalition wouldn't be putting out a hit on a cop who took a photo for a ward council race.

Despite this, the Jim Reed incident gave Ron Stih just a little more motivation as he tilted against the windmill of Coalition power in Euclid.

Stih's placing that yard sign was like planting a flag in unchartered territory under exploration.

Stih's attorney obtained a restraining order that stalled any disciplinary action from the Chief. His lawyer argued that the Hatch Act was designed to prohibit active campaigning by law enforcement.

However, according to the suit filed on behalf of the Officer Stih cabal, the Hatch Act didn't cancel a policeman's First Amendment right to express an opinion. Even under Hatch, said the Plaintiffs' complaint, a lawn sign was allowable.

With the restraining order in place, the lawn signs stayed planted. A final trial on the issue was scheduled for January after the election.

But something had happened. Stih proved that you could stick your neck out and survive to tell the tale. Chief Payne wasn't as all-powerful as everyone thought, it seemed.

This was around the time that Giunta and Rocco attended the police roll call together one morning. Roll call is the organizational meeting of all the officers about to go out on the road at the beginning of a shift.

Sensing real dissension, the pair wanted to confront Euclid's patrolmen. One of the more independent-minded men in blue referred to the visitors as "the blimp and the gimp". This rude characterization of the Mayor and the Law Director became pretty common in private talk among members of the rank and file.

Police humor can be pretty offensive. But the mere fact that a Euclid cop was willing to give voice to such a joke, even if in a whisper, meant that things were changing.

The roll call meeting produced little results as the policemen kept their opinions to themselves.

However, it was becoming apparent that cops like Ron Stih and his cohorts could challenge the machine without immediately having their heads chopped off. All the members of the police and fire departments noticed this.

All the City Hall workers noticed this.

Ron Stih's story made headlines so everybody in Euclid noticed as well. The trial court would eventually vindicate Stih long after the election was over but no one knew that in the fall of 1987.

Stih's challenge was an important moment. Some of those who had generally regarded the Coalition with fear and trepidation changed after hearing about Stih's courage. That cardboard lawn sign became a symbol for those who dared to challenge the high and mighty.

The people of Euclid were emboldened.

The Many Faces of Joe

WHAT I DETESTED MOST about the Coalition wasn't its corruption.

It was its racism.

I've mentioned their efforts to convince the white majority to perpetuate the Coalition's grip on the city in order to keep blacks out of Euclid. The Coalition knew that it couldn't legally prohibit minorities from shopping in or moving into Euclid. But they also knew that keeping Euclid unfriendly for minorities would discourage them from making the effort.

It was logical. If the whites were the dominant majority, the Coalition could win every election by convincing them that only the Coalition stood between Euclid and that word.

Integration.

The Coalition proclaimed integration evil.

To best understand the Coalition's tactics, you must examine a piece of campaign literature that has become legend in political circles. It's legend because it was one of our country's last examples of political racism actually reduced to printed form where it couldn't be denied. Copies of this campaign material have been saved by those who want to preserve the evidence.

The piece was called "The Many Faces of Joe" and was released by the Euclid Independent Coalition Party in late October of 1979, in the last days of the mayoral campaign where Joe Farrell ran against Mayor

Giunta. Jochum, as mentioned earlier, played the spoiler as the third candidate on the ballot.

The Mayor's race was boiling over with accusations as Councilman Farrell mounted a massive effort to keep Fat Tony from becoming another Coalition Mayor.

The literature was physically huge, the size of a full-page newspaper sheet. Black ink on white paper featured a sketch of the face of Joe Farrell in silhouette, reproduced several times throughout the page. This propaganda piece followed the theme of the art by asking "The many faces of Joe...which one do you know?"

It then went on to describe Joe Farrell's association with fair housing, public housing, busing of school children, federal mandates, and downtown politicians in the City of Cleveland. Joe's true stance on these matters was not accurately described but truth telling was never important to the Coalition in those days.

The Coalition knew that white Euclidians had a fear of anything even remotely associated with integration. These were the hot buttons for racists in Euclid and the Coalition was pushing all of them all at the same time. Calling someone an integrationist in Euclid was like calling a candidate a gun control advocate in rural Georgia.

The photographs in this campaign piece were especially galling. It showed a run-down residence with an old junk car, complete with flat tires and busted windows, parked in the front yard. The caption told the reader that Farrell would bring this type of housing into our city.

A second picture depicted a street of immaculate homes and manicured lawns. This gorgeous neighborhood is the kind of thing you could expect by re-electing Tony Giunta, according to the literature.

People who were paying attention might have noticed that the photo of the run-down home came from the Euclid Homes development that was owned by the city, allowed to deteriorate under Mayor Giunta's watch, a minor detail left undisclosed by the Coalition. The photograph suited their purpose in this attack piece so they used it.

The question about federal mandates concerned the application of anti-discrimination rules to recipients of federal funds. Euclid was already accepting Community Development Block Grant funds from the Department of Housing and Urban Development (HUD) by this time. Behind closed doors, Mayor Giunta derisively referred to these grants as "black" grant funds.

In addition, the giant piece neglected to mention that fair-housing was the law of the land passed by the United States Congress. Giunta and Rocco were bound by that law but this deceptive campaign material gave the impression that Farrell had to be defeated so that housing discrimination could be preserved.

The piece declared Joe guilty of tolerance by association as it described his occasional dealings with downtown politicians. "Downtown politicians" was a euphemism for black leaders who had been flexing their muscle in the City of Cleveland for several years. The document was so racist that even Joe Farrell was surprised by the blatant nature of it. Joe actually called Frank Chukayne, Giunta's campaign chairman, and threatened to call the United States Department of Justice.

Chukayne shrugged. He told Joe that there was nothing racist in it. The Coalition just wanted the people to know Joe's position on the issues. The despicable literature went to all the homes in Euclid.

Unfortunately, Euclid was at that time susceptible to such demagoguery. Mostly white Euclid was full of middle-class families who feared busing especially.

The strife and violence which occurred in Boston and other major cities over the issue of forced busing to achieve school integration had been making headlines across the nation. The Cleveland City School District was in the throes of that same controversy when "Many faces of Joe" appeared.

Euclid's ethnic population didn't take kindly to the idea that Joe believed in the constitutional protections given minorities under the Fourteenth Amendment. After all, when you let one black family move into the neighborhood, the entire area falls apart, right? Just look at those photos!

Euclid of that era was Archie Bunker territory. And the Coalition swore to keep George Jefferson out of Euclid. This historic campaign literature so enflamed racial passions that one day after its circulation, someone burned a cross on Joe Farrell's front yard around midnight. Joe and his family were terrified. They felt like a branch of the Ku Klux Klan had suddenly taken root in Euclid.

Racism in print: The Coalition goes after Joe Farrell.

That's how Joe lost. Victimized by insidious racism. Something good came of this in the end, however. The priests and ministers of Euclid were outraged by the Coalition's attempt to play the race card.

Euclid has a lot of churches. The men of the cloth united in their righteous indignation over the racist "Many Faces of Joe."

The clergy of Euclid called an emergency *ad hoc* meeting hastily organized to prepare a response. The religious leaders actually composed a letter to the citizenry titled "We were disappointed."

This letter criticized Fat Tony and the Coalition for the unchristian attitude demonstrated in "Many faces." The letter urged Euclidians to turn away from fear and prejudice and instead embrace brotherly love. It did not mention Joe or directly support his candidacy, but it was obvious that they supported Joe's more progressive approach to government.

Joe's team worked hard to get that correspondence to every household in Euclid. Newspapers all over Northeast Ohio reproduced the beautiful letter that preached equality and goodwill to all.

This didn't help Joe. In fact, it hurt him.

The old-fashioned white-majority saw the letter as confirmation of the "Many faces" attack. Euclid wasn't ready for a modern thinker. They bought into the old-Coalition racism and Joe was toast. The good part of all this was that the ministers made their hastily formed group a permanent organization. Those outraged priests and ministers called themselves the Euclid Clergy Association and they remained active after the "Many Faces" incident.

I was happy about that. I would need them around as I wandered into the same fiery furnace of Coalition politics that almost consumed my dear friend Joe Farrell.

I wondered what version of "Many faces" would be aimed at me. We braced for the worst.

I connected a garden hose to the water spigot in the front of my home.

Just in case.

Minority Report

WHILE MAYOR GIUNTA assured his coalition loyalists that he would keep the blacks out of Euclid, he realized that he had to mollify state, county, and federal officials that were concerned about what was happening in Euclid. The "Many Faces of Joe" incident had attracted significant attention, especially from the United States Department of Justice which took a dim view of racial discrimination incorporated into local government policy. Euclid was officially now under the microscope when it came to race.

Giunta seized upon the recently created federal holiday established to honor slain civil rights leader Martin Luther King as a way to deflect growing criticism of the Coalition's discriminatory practices. Giunta would attend various public services organized to pay tribute to MLK. At these events, Giunta would tell the public that he was "sensitive" to the plight of minorities in society.

Everyone who knew the Coalition knew what a joke that was.

Fat Tony never pronounced the name of Martin Luther King properly in any of his public speeches. He used to refer to the assassinated leader as Martin "Lutheran" King. Giunta feigned innocence, but it was generally understood that the mispronunciation served as a coded message to the segregationists: I am still one of you.

Giunta also opposed an organization called Citizens For Block Grant Compliance. With Euclid taking full advantage of new federal grants designed to assist municipal governments, the mayor refused to certify that his government would comply with federal regulations related to fair housing, All he had to do was sign a form agreeing that housing discrimination based on race was not to be tolerated. He couldn't bring himself to do it and the citizen group took him to court for violating federal law.

The fact is that Tony showed nothing but contempt for minorities privately while at best taking only a patronizing attitude publicly. Illustrative of this point was the hiring policy at City Hall. Giunta used to proclaim that his administration hired blacks on a regular basis. Eight percent of city workers were African-American, he would point out. Giunta was accurate in this remark but there was more to the story.

All eight percent worked in the trash collection division of the city. The Coalition made it very clear: If you wanted a city job and you were black, you had to haul trash. The job of garbageman was the only one available to minorities.

The policy was demeaning. In fact, to preserve the racial purity of the remainder of city hall, not one white person worked as a trash collector. The pay was the lowest of any city job and the working conditions were deplorable.

In essence, Mayor Giunta saved money by running a plantation, white overseers monitoring black workers picking up garbage for proper white folk. This had to change. A good city job could be a path to upward mobility but somebody had to stop the Coalition's attempt to keep African-Americans in their place.

I also knew that hiring minorities in safety, finance, and all the other departments would have tremendous symbolic value. It would be a proclamation that Jim Crow was dead. I longed for the chance to officiate at the funeral.

The difficulty lay in the politics. Without question, in the homes of white, narrow-minded old timers, my concept of a fair, racially-neutral City Hall was anathema. I was in danger of playing right into the hands of my enemies.

My campaign had to be more than just about changing the leadership. Could I also change the hearts of our citizenry?

I realized that I was faced with perhaps the greatest leadership challenge: leading the people to a place they don't want to go to begin with. Lincoln, Wilson, and FDR took our nation reluctantly into war. Could I be elected while preaching the gospel of compassion and justice to Tony's retinue of bigots?

I was determined to convince voters that honest, efficient government was on its way if Lynch were elected and that the equal opportunity which accompanied it would not spell the ruin of our community.

This looked like a tall order in the Euclid of 1987, but I could tell as I stood on front stoops all over town that Euclid was at a tipping point in terms of social thought. Our city needed a little push and ever so gently, I was pushing.

CHAPTER TWENTY-FIVE

Limping Along

NANCY AND I STRUGGLED to have some kind of normal life as the campaign of 1987 continued.

It was difficult because I was pounding the pavement with the door knocking every single day, Saturday and Sunday included.

Nancy kept things organized. She sent me off to do the grunt work on the sidewalk as she kept tabs on volunteers, events, printing literature, lawn signs, and the campaign budget.

She kept our family organized as well. Our son Scott had been born in July of 1985 and his sister Bridget came along almost exactly one year later in July of 1986.

As August of 1987 wound down, I was the only opponent facing Mayor Giunta and I felt like I had a target on my back.

Nancy was chasing two small children in between running my campaign, with daddy absent during almost every bit of daylight.

Nancy and I set aside Sunday mornings as a time for much-needed spirituality and recreation. So we set off for Mass early every seventh day with little Scotty and Bridget in tow. We were exhausted, but those Sunday mornings gave us a little respite from the worries about the Coalition's next strike. After Mass ended, we would change clothes and head to Euclid Memorial Park for a softball game.

I loved softball. I was never a great athlete, but I relished being a weekend warrior for those Sunday morning battles on the diamond.

Sunday mornings allowed us to focus on something nonpolitical for a while. We needed the break.

I wasn't much of a hitter, but I was fast and pretty good with the glove. I enjoyed those games, parked in right field, waiting to turn some hotshot's chance at a double or home run into a loud out.

Nobody expects the right fielder to be very good. I specialized in surprising teams by ranging far past the first base line to snag a foul ball. Lots of promising at-bats ended when I came up with an unexpected catch. My technique lacked Joe DiMaggio's grace, but my teammates enjoyed my aggressive outfield play.

Our team was called Major Construction, sponsored by my Slovenian builder brother-in-law Bill "Major" Barbis.

The team's manager and second baseman was another brother-in-law, Kevin Cawneen. Kevin was an accountant for British Petroleum, a Fortune 500 Corporation. He was no stranger to pressure.

He understood me. He always kept me in the lineup because he knew I needed the therapeutic effect of these games. As the second baseman, he was the one who stepped out onto the edge of the outfield grass to receive my relay throw after someone hit a single to right. It was great to have his friendly Irish face on the diamond with me.

Our uniforms were white with red lettering and red short sleeves. We played in the B division of the 35 and under league, not for the high caliber players. Most of us were just playing ball so that we could get some exercise.

The young studs of the town played during the week at night. Now that was serious ball. Euclid was known for its outstanding weeknight softball teams that frequently played for national titles.

Our team wasn't terrible, but we weren't great either. Once the season started, we never practiced. Just a bunch of guys having fun, occasionally convening at someone's house for a barbecue.

To me, the definition of happiness was basking in the sun in right field, Nancy and the kids in the stands waiting to see if the ball came in dad's direction.

Why this digression into the seemingly irrelevant subject of my mediocre career in Sunday morning softball? Well, something happened which shook me and my family to the core.

During the last week of August, my left arm went limp. I mean, it just hung there at my side. I couldn't raise it. If you've ever seen Senator Bob Dole on television, you've noticed his war injuries force him to shake hands from the left side. His right arm is useless. That's what I experienced on my left side. This terrified me.

I have an older brother, Bob, who contracted Guillain-Barré syndrome years earlier. Guillain-Barré is a form of virus that attacks the spinal cord, leaving permanent damage in its wake. My brother remains a quadriplegic to this day as a result of the deadly condition.

Here I was in the prime of life in the middle of the fight of my life and now this?

I went to see a neurologist. He ran some initial tests. Not Lou Gehrig's disease.

Not multiple sclerosis. And thankfully, not Guillain-Barré syndrome.

What then?

He didn't know.

He told me to come back in two weeks if the arm didn't come back to life by then. We'll run more tests at that time to get to the bottom of the problem.

He guessed that somehow I had pinched a nerve in my neck, causing paralysis in the left arm. Scared as hell, I continued the campaign knocking on doors. No one outside of my immediate family knew my problem. Thankfully, I could continue shaking hands (I was right-handed) and the disability went undetected.

I sat out the next ballgame on Sunday. The following week, we were in a playoff game but we were also shorthanded. I had to play.

Kevin told the player in right center (softball teams have four outfielders) to cover for me.

Understand my situation. Here I stood in right field, glove on my left hand. Unable to raise that glove to catch anything. With my condition a secret and other outfielders shifting to cover my territory, I might fake my way through the game.

Batting was easier as I could grab a bat with my left hand and use my right arm to raise the bat. No hitting power, but I might be able to beat out a slow grounder.

What happened next became the stuff of softball legend in the Euclid amateur division.

Some bruiser from the opposition lifted a ball deep to right field. Nobody could get close to this one except for me. I ran full tilt.

I turned all the burners on high and actually began to catch up to the rocket ball. The small crowd looked on quizzically as I approached intersecting with the ball beginning its downward descent. Why isn't he raising his glove? Raise the glove!

I couldn't. Arm wouldn't budge!

It was all happening in slow motion right in front of me.

Back to home plate, I dove, stretching my frame to its full 5'11" length.

My Rawlings big basket mitt dangling down by my left thigh.

Instinctively, I stuck out my right hand.

My bare right hand.

The potential home run ball fell safely into my palm.

As I got up off the turf, the umpire raised his right hand to signal a clean catch for the third out. The official scorer, Frankie Snyder, asked me why I had to do things the hard way. He'd never seen anything like it, he said.

I just smiled. So did Kevin and Nancy. Everyone else who witnessed the bizarre play just scratched their heads.

That night, my arm sprang back to life.

I talked to the neurologist the next day. Stress can cause these things, he said. He wondered if I'd been under any stress. Just a bit, I told him.

The grind of the campaign resumed, but the left arm paralysis never returned. Nancy and I felt like we'd experienced just about the entire range of human emotion. Yes, we were both stressed out. But we leaned on each other and felt a special bond.

We drew strength from the knowledge that we'd be together, no matter what life threw at us. No matter what the Coalition threw at us.

What else could happen?

No Swimming

THE CONTROVERSY over the wastewater sludge plant incinerator seemed reason enough to deny me the chairmanship of the Wastewater Committee.

However, about sixty days before the election, I stumbled across a much darker secret.

The City of Euclid, under Mayor's Giunta's reign, had been sued by the Environmental Protection Agency for around $400 million in fines and penalties for polluting Lake Erie. It had something to do with the City's wastewater treatment plant.

This 1950s-era sewage plant would collect the wastewater sewage from all the toilets and sinks in the city, eliminating the pollutants before sending the treated and hopefully purified water back into the great Lake Erie.

The water sent back out into the lake after treatment is called effluent, and the plant's location right on the Lake Erie shoreline meant it was well-positioned to pipe the effluent back into one of the world's great lakes.

The EPA lawsuit had been described to city Council as a "purely technical" issue, nothing to worry about. Rocco portrayed the EPA as a bunch of pointy-headed technocrats trying to squeeze money from the city over picayune federal regulations. Giunta and Rocco assured us that the city was smoothly and efficiently filtering out the sewage before sending the effluent into Erie.

Being an attorney has its advantages. I began researching the EPA allegations, finally getting my hands on the original lawsuit filed against the municipality.

It was stunning.

Euclid, during heavy rainstorms, was sending millions of gallons of raw untreated sewage directly into the blue waters of Erie. Human fecal matter from the neighborhood commodes was making its way straight into these pristine waters. Here's how it happened, over and over again, perhaps as many as 20 or 30 times a year.

Euclid toilets empty into a sanitary sewer system that flows into the wastewater treatment plant on Lake Erie at the intersection of Lakeshore Boulevard and East 222nd Street. Most days, the plant filters, clarifies, and chlorinates with positive results. You have a pretty healthy effluent return to the lake while the nasty pollutants are pumped to the sludge incinerator about two miles further south.

Here's the problem. Storm drains in about 40% of the homes and businesses were improperly tied into the sanitary system instead of the storm system designed to carry clean rainwater out to the lake.

With so many storm drains connected to the sanitary system, a heavy rain sends way too much water into the wastewater treatment plant. In fact, a major storm essentially floods out the plant, potentially causing a disgusting backup into the basements of Euclid homeowners.

In these heavy rainfall events, the city of Euclid opened up the water release doors into Lake Erie. In essence, the city would empty out the plant to stop it from flooding and to stop it from backing up into basements. Euclid was literally "opening the floodgates."

Now if the open floodgates sent only storm water into the lake, it wouldn't be so bad. But the plant was always full of sanitary waste to begin with, so opening the floodgates was the equivalent of a giant toilet flushing after you've had a nasty bout with diarrhea.

The disgusting results were as you can imagine. Beaches were closed because of the dangerous fecal content. Condoms and toilet paper washed up on shore. A deluge in Euclid would create a health disaster. The Coalition and Rocco knew about this problem for years, but they chose to ignore it, unleashing these epic attacks on the environment.

The cross connections of storm lines into the sanitary sewers took place under the watch of City of Euclid inspectors who should have been making certain that builders properly connected the various sewer lines. Unfortunately, most of these inspectors were Coalition political hacks, sleeping on the job while one storm line after another was connected to the sanitary system.

Who knows how many inspectors were overlooking the improper connections in return for a wad of cash from a builder who could save a few bucks with the cross connection? After all, if a sanitary line was nearby, wouldn't it be cheaper to tie in there as opposed to running a longer pipe out to the storm line? Once the pipes were buried in the earth, who would know the difference? Lake Erie was being destroyed by political cronyism.

The City of Euclid needed a plan to fix the problem. But Giunta and Rocco couldn't quite embrace a new plan without admitting the Coalition's complicity in creating the problem to begin with.

Apart from the danger to health and the environment, there was a horrible impact on the recreation and fishing industries on Lake Erie. Northeast Ohio boasts more boating licenses per capita than almost any place in the world. Lake Erie walleye is perhaps to Cleveland what clam chowder is to Boston. It's our signature native dish.

The Euclid segment of Erie, the grand dame of Northeast Ohio, was full of crap. So were Giunta and Rocco, and I was determined to win the election so we could face up to the problem and fix it. The challenge was in coming up with an explanation voters could understand. This was an important issue but it was extremely complex.

Every time I flushed the toilet, I thought about what was happening and vowed to set things right if the voters would give me a chance. I began to address the problem in campaign literature and on the stump.

Unfortunately, it was hard to effectively communicate the details of the problem without losing my audience after a few minutes.

Regardless, I knew that I would have to take drastic action to protect the lake if I ever got the chance to sit in the Mayor's seat.

My mother used to draw sketches of King Neptune, God of the Sea, when I was a kid. Maybe he would thrust his trident at Giunta's campaign so that I could do something to protect the water.

CHAPTER TWENTY-SEVEN

The Firefighters

THE EUCLID FIREFIGHTERS and Euclid police were the biggest and most powerful unions in the City of Euclid. But Giunta and the Coalition were at loggerheads with the police and firemen.

The reason was no mystery. The Coalition was always fighting pay raises for the safety forces.

Why?

The answer lies in the politics of the city government. Mayor Giunta used hiring as a powerful political weapon. He was constantly creating new positions to add to his army of campaign workers.

The police and fire departments, however, required a civil service test as the core of the hiring process. The only pathway to employment in the city's safety forces was through this competitive testing.

In other words, Giunta was powerless to influence police and fire department hiring. The jobs there went to the highest scores. Consequently, there was no political benefit for the Coalition in maintaining the budgets in police and fire.

For this reason, Giunta tended to favor fattening the budgets in the departments where he had the power to hire anyone he wanted. The policemen and firefighters saw this and pushed hard for pay increases commensurate with the largess heaped on the departments populated by political hires.

But the Coalition refused to give ground. The funding of non-civil service areas was precious to this government where political patronage was the lifeblood for the Giunta, Rocco, and Chukayne triumvirate.

Year after year, the scenario repeated itself. The Coalition restricted wages for police and fire while the safety unions clawed and scratched their way through one wage arbitration after another.

The rank and file of the firefighters became disgusted with Giunta and his cronies. They were hungry for alternative leadership in government. All they needed was someone to convince them that somebody, anybody, had a chance to defeat the machine.

That's why I knew the meeting in my dining room with the president and vice-president of the Euclid Firefighters Union was a game changer.

Bernie Harchar was president and Pat Boyce was vice-president. These two were somewhat of an odd couple.

Bernie was detail oriented, always studying the fine points of the fire contract. He calculated and compared wage rates, memorizing relevant charts and projections. He was trim with dark hair cut short in a marine style flat top. His compact neat appearance was consistent with his no nonsense analytical approach to his duties as president of the union.

Bernie's sidekick, Union Vice-President Pat Boyce, was a bear of a man with big hands and a bigger heart. He loved to tell a joke, then laugh with you, guffawing loudly at his own punchlines. Pat enjoyed holding meetings at a local tavern named Skinny's, where the beer flowed freely and hoagie sandwiches were served to all. Few who patronized Skinny's remained skinny for long. Pat lived life large.

The fire union membership had faith in these two. They knew Bernie had the brains to follow the right strategy and Boyce had the heart to protect their families. In essence, Bernie and Pat were trusted and loved. If these two got behind a candidate, the firefighters would follow.

The Firefighters Union Leadership

Bernie Harchar was the brain...   *.... and Pat Boyce was the heart.*

To my delight, Bernie and Pat were so angry with Giunta and the Coalition that I merely had to convince them that I was sincere and willing to work hard to defeat the enemy. They agreed to support me.

The three of us developed into a brotherhood on a mission. These two men rolled up their sleeves and jumped right into the trenches with me.

From that first discussion in June of 1987 forward, we met at my home once each week to update each other on our efforts.

What did the firefighters do? Plenty.

When Bernie and Pat signaled their troops to back Lynch for Mayor, a force of firefighter families began the drumbeat for my candidacy.

Chief George Langa ran the fire department, but he took a much more passive role in the Coalition government in comparison to Chief Payne at police headquarters. Langa just did his job quietly and let Payne grab all the limelight. He saw the injustice in the depressed pay for his men but he didn't have the force of personality to be able to challenge Giunta and Rocco. Langa was happy just to keep out of their way.

When it was obvious that Harchar and Boyce were going to lead their troops in a charge to put Lynch in the mayor's seat, Langa called the pair into his office. He told them that he admired their guts and that the department would do nothing to inhibit their right of free speech.

Chief George Langa: he was willing to look the other way.

He did however, ask them one favor. Just to keep him out of trouble with Giunta and Rocco, he wanted firefighters with a Lynch For Mayor bumper sticker on the rear bumper of their cars to back into their assigned parking. This would reduce the chance that the mayor or the law director would notice. After all, reasoned Langa, why stick it in the mayor's face?

Harchar and Boyce readily agreed. The chief was turning out to be reasonable. As I would learn later, Langa was disenchanted with the Coalition, especially under Rocco's reign. Bernie whispered his suspicion that Langa was quietly in the Lynch camp.

In a strange twist, the Coalition suffered from a local ordinance it had promoted for years: forced city residency for safety forces. Because of the residency requirement, Giunta guaranteed that sprinkled throughout neighborhoods in Euclid were firefighter families, exuberantly telling neighbors and friends to join with them to end the half-century dictatorial grip the Coalition had on the community.

These firefighters talked about the election at every opportunity.

Suddenly, I had over 100 public relations agents singing my praises. They convinced ordinary citizens that it was time to topple the old regime. The firefighters also helped me obtain lawn sign locations. This gave me an effective ground game. Essentially, the fire union members provided me with workers that I just didn't otherwise have.

True, Giunta had workers of his own in the families of those hired as political patronage.

Here was the difference. Giunta's campaign workers did indeed pass out literature and make phone calls. But they campaigned for Tony because Tony told them that they owed it to him. In contrast, my army of firefighters worked to elect me for a different reason. They gave me their time because they wanted to.

The difference between soldiers forced into conscription and warriors united by a noble cause is the difference between night and day. And, I hoped, the difference between winning and losing.

Inspired by leadership from Pat and Bernie, this battalion of men enthusiastically went to war for my election. They believed in me. Many of the firefighters used their free time to make Lynch for Mayor cold calls to voters from a phone bank set up at the local union hall.

Giunta alienated the firefighters and unintentionally provided me with scores of families converted into powerful allies. In a local election, nothing is more potent than the words of motivated citizens spoken in living rooms, church lobbies, and at potluck dinners.

The Lynch campaign needed a Marine landing and the firefighters became the Marines.

Semper Fi.

CHAPTER TWENTY-EIGHT

Lawyer Bucks System

A FEW WEEKS BEFORE ELECTION DAY, the Giunta campaign ran a full page ad in the newspaper. It was captioned "Those who love Euclid support Tony Giunta".

Below that headline ran the names of all the people who had publicly endorsed Mayor Giunta. The list of names was gargantuan.

About 300 people were listed, including doctors, lawyers, insurance brokers, accountants, and engineers. These were the crème de la crème of our community.

The presidents of every fraternal organization in Euclid from the Elks to the Knights of Columbus were also listed, proclaiming their allegiance to the Coalition standard bearer.

What made it brilliant was that the reader was bound to find someone's name on that list that they knew and respected. It's part of that six degrees of separation theory.

This concept tells us that someone you know knows someone else who is familiar with another person who was friends with another individual who associates with another person whose barber cuts the hair of the President of the United States.

This makes sense.

It's a simple permutation. You know enough folks such that you are connected to everyone else in the world through this chain of association. By publishing this comprehensive list of local luminaries, every voter was likely to find a familiar name.

If Uncle Jack loves Tony, then I'll vote for him too, by golly.

I felt defeated when I saw that advertisement. There were so many talented people I knew as smart and responsible, I began to doubt myself.

If the gifted thinkers view Tony as good for our city, then who was I to question their judgment? After all, what did I really know about running a $40 million operation? How could I master the complexities?

Rocco may have been a schemer, but he was intelligent and capable.

I felt like a mouse among lions.

Insignificant.

An asterisk footnote to the main body of the text. And that text was the long proud history of the Euclid Independent Coalition Party.

Then I got an interesting phone call. It was attorney Mike Lavigna. I didn't know him personally. His name had been listed in the famous advertisement along with the rest of the elite standing in Tony's corner.

Lavigna had been practicing law in Euclid for 15 years and had become one of the leaders in the local Bar Association. The public knew him. He was a leading citizen: someone people listen to.

But he called for a reason. Something was troubling him. The Coalition had not bothered to get his permission to include his name in the advertisement.

Sure he had purchased tickets to Coalition events in the past. So had everyone else in and around Euclid.

But he had not publicly endorsed Tony Giunta for Mayor. Apparently, the Coalition just assumed Mike Lavigna was on board. After all, who wouldn't be?

Mike called just to let me know the truth. In fact, he was a little angry at the presumptuousness of the powerful Coalition. He wanted me to know that out of a sense of fairness to me.

I appreciated that. Before hanging up, I asked him a tough question. Would he be willing to publicly correct the record? Tell the world that the list contained a mistake? That Mike Lavigna was not endorsing Tony and that they never even obtained permission to publish his name?

Mike asked for a day to think this over. It was one thing to privately tell me what happened. It was another to put himself in harm's way.

Mike Lavigna practiced law in the courtroom of Judge Robert F. "Stick' em" Niccum. Publicly decrying Coalition tactics was not going to increase his client base. Crazy Judge Niccum was bound to seek revenge by punishing Lavigna's clients.

I could tell, however, that Mike believed in justice, even the political kind. I think he saw the advertisement with the imposing list of names as a sort of "piling on" against another candidate about to get creamed by the big machine.

The Coalition had all the advantages without cheating, he reasoned. Why resort to including names without permission?

Mike called back the next day. He was in.

He had a plan. He contacted the newspaper where the original ad appeared. He insisted they publish his letter to the editor exposing the outrage of Tony using Mike's name without first seeking Mike's approval.

The paper agreed. Mike's letter appeared in a prominent place in the next edition of the *Euclid News Journal*. In the letter, Mike did not endorse me. He didn't have to.

He criticized Tony's campaign for the unauthorized use of his name. He said Tony was dishonest in presenting the list of supporters. That list was a lie as far as he was concerned. Mike expressed indignation.

I know people saw Mike's letter because I was getting feedback in the last few neighborhoods of my doorknocking. People didn't like Tony's tactics.

But would this help me obtain an electoral overthrow? Mike Lavigna's courage gave us a little more hope.

CHAPTER TWENTY-NINE

Losing a Few Pounds

ONE DAY I wrapped up my doorknocking and headed home.

It was around 6 PM and I noticed an announcement on the reader board in front of the Euclid Presbyterian Church.

This church was headed up by a pastor involved in community affairs. He frequently came to Council meetings to remind us of the important social issues in town. His big project was the Euclid Hunger Center where citizens could drop off non-perishables or make donations.

The good pastor was always urging Euclid citizens to help those in need, especially those in the inner city in Cleveland.

So I had a pretty good feeling when I saw "Mayoral Forum Tonight" on the prominent reader board in the front yard of the church. I knew the church pastor was a fair man and I'd be given a fair shake in a candidate night run by the church. I was especially excited because this forum, according to the announcement board, did not involve City Council.

Without the distraction of the City Council candidates, I could really focus the audience's attention on the important issues in the Mayor's race.

What bothered me was what appeared to be a lack of organization in my own campaign. I did not have this event on my calendar. It's a little disconcerting when a mayoral forum is discovered as I'm driving home on the day of the event. What would've happened if I had taken another route home?

I dashed to my house for a quick bite. Nancy was my campaign manager and she swore up and down that she had received no notice of the event at the Presbyterian Church.

I knew she was right. She was meticulous about checking the mail for campaign related activities and putting them on my calendar. Sometimes I had to go to multiple events but Nancy always kept things organized. She hated surprises and was always prepared.

We didn't have a sitter, so I went to the church for the 7 PM meeting all by myself. I got there about 10 minutes before seven and headed to the front of the room where there was a podium, along with a six-foot long folding table with three folding chairs behind the table.

The basement meeting room of the church held about 75 people. Pretty small crowd.

Behind the podium an eight foot long felt banner announced that this was not a church sponsored event. The banner read T.O.P.S. in big red letters on a yellow field.

TOPS stands for Take Off Pounds Sensibly.

It was a weight-loss group! Okay I said to myself, I get it. Political awareness was important for everybody and I found it kind of cool to think a weight-loss club wanted to sponsor a debate for mayoral candidates.

I reviewed my notes as the membership slowly filled the seats in the audience. Tony came in next and we both took seats at the chairs behind the long table. I waited for my turn at the podium.

They began with the Pledge of Allegiance and the club president, a short white-haired lady in a blue dress, reviewed a list of upcoming events. I looked at Tony sitting next to me, a smug expression on his face.

Madam President, still at the podium, then made a stunning announcement.

"Mr. Lynch, would you please leave?"

What?

"Mr. Lynch, please leave because you've not been invited."

Say what?

Here we were, just 19 days before an election to determine the leader of our city and this club was having a forum inviting only one of the two candidates? Yup.

I gathered my notes together. Then I had to cross to the back of the room to get my coat. Then back to the front of the room to the stairs, up to the exit, and finally out of the building into the parking lot.

I felt like I was moving in slow motion, all 76 pairs of eyes on me as I left their meeting somewhat confused and embarrassed.

And also weirdly ashamed. How could I be so stupid?

I felt like a circus freak.

What did they possibly think about some young kid who showed up uninvited?

Tony was their guy, and I was horning in on their chance to show him how much they loved him.

I could feel the blood rush to my head as I got back into my car.

What just happened?

I knew what just happened. The spectacle of my ignominious ejection from the meeting must have destroyed any chance I had with any uncommitted voters that might have been in the room that night.

After all, TOPS was a private club. They're not required to be fair. They can take sides if they want to.

And that night, they wanted to.

This was a real low point for me. I just drove around the city for about 20 minutes.

Filled with self-doubt.

Filled with self-pity.

Nancy was surprised to see me when I came home so early. I told her what happened and she gave me a long hug.

Then she laughed.

Then I laughed.

We laughed together: Fat Tony, with his rotund figure, needed TOPS a lot more than I did. Unfortunately, I needed every vote I could scavenge up if I were to have a chance on election day. I called Joe Farrell.

He told me that the sun would come up the next morning and that I should forget about the whole thing.

The sun did indeed come up the next day, but Joe was wrong about one thing. I didn't forget.

While it was laughable, it still didn't seem fair. The Coalition controlled everything.

Including the politicized agenda for the meeting of a weight-loss club. This club was willing to tip the scales in Tony's favor, pun intended.

Now that's power.

CHAPTER THIRTY

Louie Paroska

LOUIE PAROSKA worked for the City of Euclid in the motor maintenance department in 1987. He was indispensable.

That's because Louie was mechanically inclined, so much so that there were few devices from toasters to tow motors that he couldn't completely disassemble and put back together again in perfect working order.

He was one of those mechanical geniuses who had an intuitive sense about the way gears, pistons, and fan belts powered equipment in the modern industrial age. His skill with a toolbox in the face of engine failure from police cars to hook and ladders made him the focus of the motor maintenance department's ability to keep the fleet going.

What made Louie especially valuable was his ability to diagnose a problem and then go into the city's machine shop where he would manufacture a metal flange or some other part needed for the repair.

Louie saved the city hundreds of thousands of dollars because his knowledge, experience, and know-how allowed him to repair vehicles and equipment that would otherwise have been sent off to a private commercial shop.

Jerry Akos, the foreman of motor maintenance, made sure that all the big jobs passed muster with Louie before they went back on the road. Even more remarkable was Louie's importance in the motor maintenance department in the face of his physical limitations.

Years before joining the City of Euclid, Louie had been the victim of a terrible accident while working at a butcher shop.

At age 17, Louie lost his left hand in a meat grinder that kicked back into gear while Louie was fixing a broken circuit. But the man with only one hand may have been the most dexterous and skillful mechanic in the state of Ohio.

Other guys in the department called him "the surgeon" because of the miraculous way he brought back to life complex devices that other mechanics would have shipped off to the junkyard.

Louie also had a very gruff exterior. He wouldn't put up with baloney from anybody. He was even known to talk back to his bosses on occasion when he thought workers were being treated unfairly.

Despite this, his superiors never made Louie the target of discipline. They knew that Louie Paroska knew more about the repair of diesel and gas engines than all of them put together. Motor maintenance supervisors were willing to put up with Louie's rough edges in order to keep municipal equipment running without spending a fortune.

Louie's legendary mechanical ability was common knowledge, and even Mayor Giunta realized his value. The City of Euclid had money problems and the last thing the Mayor needed was a motor maintenance budget that would balloon if Louie Paroska left that department.

Louis Paroska

Of course I didn't know any of that in April 1987 when Louie Paroska left a message one night on the answering machine in my law office. Louie wanted to meet me in a private place so he could tell me about the Coalition government. He wanted to help me in my campaign.

We went to a small diner in Richmond Heights, a city just south of Euclid, and he told me his story. Louie had been hired by the Coalition with the understanding that Louie and his entire family had signed on to be loyal soldiers for the political needs of the Coalition.

That meant distributing literature, making phone calls, and most importantly, buying tickets to and attending the multitude of Coalition fundraising events throughout the year.

It was like paying tribute to Caesar. All the Coalition events were mandatory for city workers that wanted to keep their jobs.

Louie played ball during the first five or six years of his employment. But he eventually realized that his mechanical skills made him virtually irreplaceable. So he began to speak up.

Most of the workers in motor maintenance were political hires who could do little more than change oil and replace batteries. Louie worked hard for the city and he was sincere in his effort to keep the city equipment in good shape at minimal cost. With Louie supervising, even the political hacks in that department could get the work done if they followed Louie's direction.

Louie took his responsibilities seriously because of the important services made possible for the citizens when equipment was kept in tip-top shape. He knew that ambulances, firepumpers, and police cars were essential components in providing safety to families throughout Euclid that were not much unlike his own.

He told me that the snowdrifts of January and February in Northeast Ohio were no match for the battalions of snowplow trucks that he kept running. This was a man who was proud of his important work.

But he had contacted me because he was sick of political pressure from the Coalition. Louie talked to me about creating an environment for city workers where the only thing that mattered was merit and hard work.

He told me of workers afraid to resist the political servitude imposed on those receiving a paycheck from the municipal corporation.

Louie wanted to know if I would be willing to be a mayor who could set people free from the burden of fealty to the politicians. To a great extent, it was about money. Louie was grateful to have a job, but he felt working hard and saving the city money should be enough.

The good pay and good benefits were diminished in value because the requirement to buy tickets to Coalition events was in a sense a form of taxation on city employment. Louie told me that pay raises didn't mean very much for laborers in the Euclid city government because they were consumed by this mandatory tithing to the hungry political beast.

He looked me in the eye with those clear blue eyes and asked me if I would be different. I told him that I would be different and that a new day would dawn for these workers. He believed me and shook my hand.

Thus began a long lasting friendship with this crusty mechanical genius. As the campaign progressed, he would report back to me after attending Coalition organizational meetings.

I guess you could say he was kind of a mole, but that really isn't accurate. A mole is someone who pretends to be a loyal supporter of one side when he is actually a spy for the other.

Louie Paroska told his bosses that he didn't like the political requirements of a city job. He wasn't pretending to be loyal. Louie's supervisors listened to his grousing and dismissed it as part of his curmudgeonly personality.

Louie blowing off steam wasn't unusual, and none of them suspected that he quietly became an important supporter of the Lynch campaign. Louie and I would get together regularly for coffee, holding clandestine meetings at the home of someone where no suspicion would be created. This provided me with some minor intelligence when it came to Rocco's intentions.

Minor because Rocco and Giunta weren't about to unveil details of their game plan in meetings intended to organize literature drops. Louie really didn't have access to inside information.

But what Louie did do was of tremendous value for my campaign. He spread the word that liberty was just around the corner. He told city workers to stand up for themselves in the building, recreation, waste water, streets, and parks departments. His message penetrated wherever city laborers suffered under the yoke of mandatory political activity.

Almost every city department had to communicate with motor maintenance somewhere along the way in order to make sure that their equipment was up to snuff. Louie Paroska was quietly broadcasting my message to the rank and file.

He was beating the drum and getting away with it.

Fat Tony, I'm sure, heard about these efforts, but held back, not sure what to make of the strange firebrand with one hand. Right under the nose of Commandant Chukayne, the inmates stood at attention while secretly whispering about their plans for a way to break out of this prison camp.

It would be tough for me to assemble campaign workers in numbers commensurate with the legions forced to undertake the grunt work for Fat Tony's campaign. But because of Louie Paroska, those selfsame workers were doing plenty to offset the Coalition literature they were delivering throughout the city. Because of Louie, they were circulating the battle cry of revolution. They were telling people to vote for Lynch.

I left those meetings with Louie with an overwhelming sense of responsibility. If I lost this election, Louie Paroska would surely lose his job, despite his mechanical skill.

I needed to win for the sake of the city workers and their families. I needed to win for Louie.

CHAPTER THIRTY-ONE

Halloween

ONE OF THE BIGGEST CHALLENGES we had was getting voter attention during the campaign.

Television was out of the question.

Too expensive.

Although the door-to-door work I was doing was effective, we needed something to give voters one last reminder that there was a viable alternative for the city's future. The problem was cutting through all the clutter and the noise of the last days of the campaign.

On the ballot that November were races for Mayor, all nine council seats, school board positions, five state constitutional issues, and three tax questions. Voters were inundated with campaign messages as October began closing in on November.

How could we get folks to pay attention, especially this late in the game?

The mail came in one Saturday morning and I noticed Nancy was excited about a wedding invitation. In fact, Nancy had tossed the other mail aside so she could focus on the request for our attendance at the nuptials of a friend. Everyone loves to be invited to a party or to some exciting event.

And everybody loves to find that invitation in the mail mixed in with all the mundane correspondence and bills. So what would happen if your mailbox was crammed with six or seven varieties of campaign literature, a reminder from your mortgage company, a water department notice, and a clearly marked personal invitation to something special?

You know what you would open first.

So we prepared one last mailing, sent first class. That's pricey, but it had to look real.

We designed a satin ivory envelope 4-inches long and 4-inches wide on heavy bond paper. It didn't look like political material.

In the upper left-hand corner, there was a friendly jack-o'-lantern in orange ink. Underneath the pumpkin were the words "You Are Invited".

You had to open the envelope to see what you were invited to. Inside it read "Yes, you are invited to change the direction of your city. Save the future of Euclid by electing David M. Lynch Mayor on November 3."

Mayor Giunta's people complained. They said it was wrong to trick people into opening our campaign piece.

It was a little cheesy. But it worked. That's why the Coalition was perturbed. They didn't think of it. Every registered voter opened the highly-attractive invitation.

A lot of people thought it was clever. Clever because everyone was reading about me, just before election day.

The Coalition's carping about our little Halloween surprise maneuver did not garner much sympathy. The truth is that the Coalition wasn't really worried. They knew that in Euclid, the Coalition always prevails.

A little pretend pumpkin party wasn't going to cause Giunta and Rocco to even break a sweat. They intended to keep the Coalition steamroller moving forward in first gear.

Slowly but surely our campaign team was crawling toward the finish line. Election day couldn't come soon enough.

We began to feel spent.

CHAPTER THIRTY-TWO

Slovenian

EUCLID IN 1987 had a very ethnic population.

By far, the most dominant ethnic group in the city were the Slovenian-Americans. In fact, our suburb had the second-highest concentration of persons of Slovenian descent of anyplace in the world. Only the capital of Slovenia itself in Europe, a little town called Ljubljana (pronounced "Lub-lá-ná) could boast that it had more of these hard-working, God-fearing people.

Euclid even had a street named Ljubljana. Slovenians were such a significant part of the Euclid tapestry that throughout our neighborhoods, discussions at the kitchen table were conducted in the mother tongue. English was a second language by choice as many households cherished anything that helped them connect with the homeland back in Europe.

Right in the heart of the City of Euclid, you could find the Slovenian Society Home, also known as Recher (pronounced "Rayer") Hall. This was a large complex that housed a grand banquet room along with a private club where members could while away the hours having a beer and a Slovenian sausage sandwich.

The Slovenian home featured Balinca (pronounced "Bo-leen-suh") courts where a form of bocce ball could be played. It's a cross between shuffleboard and bowling using several softball-sized wooden balls.

If you wanted to succeed in Euclid politics, you had to win over the Slovenian community.

When I ran for city Council in 1985 against George Carson, I got strange looks when this young Irishman approached the secretary in the office of the Slovenian Society Home. The elderly woman behind the desk took my money and I proudly studied my new membership card. The card permitted me to participate in all club activities and even sit at the bar with the other members to exchange opinions on the issues of the day.

What made George Carson such a formidable opponent back in 1985 was the fact that the Slovenian Society Home had named Carson the Slovenian Man of the Year.

Some political experts concluded that winning the Slovenian vote was all that one needed to prevail in any election in Euclid.

At first, I felt out of place pursuing votes in this atmosphere that seemed so strange to me. But I kept at it, going to as many events at Recher Hall as I could and trying to integrate myself into the Slovenian culture.

The undisputed leader of the Slovenians in Euclid was a popular radio host by the name of Tony Petkovsek. Tony's show came on the air at 3 o'clock in the afternoon seven days a week on WELW radio. Slovenian-Americans throughout Northeast Ohio listened religiously as Tony was their lifeline to the old country. Petkovsek was the voice of Slovenian-America and WELW was the flagship station for Slovenian music and news.

Petkovsek's program featured reports from Europe, along with stories of the endeavors of Slovenian-Americans in the United States. However, the real staple of the program was polka bands with their latest releases becoming hits because Tony decided to play these records on his show.

When it came to politics and polka music, Tony Petkovsek was a kingmaker. When Tony attended big events at the Slovenian Society Home, people crowded around just to get a glimpse of him. Tony's fans worshipped him. If you wanted to hold public office in Euclid, or launch a polka band in Cleveland, Tony's treatment of your career could make or break you.

Tony Petkovsek takes a break during a broadcast. Political hopefuls coveted his endorsement and musical careers blossomed if you made his play list.

Fortunately for me in 1985, Tony allowed me to buy commercial time on his show during the campaign. Even though Tony was personally behind George Carson, he played the commercial that I had produced to promote my campaign for city council. This was significant because my building contractor brother-in-law Bill Barbis read the script perfectly where he identified himself as a Slovenian-American asking voters to support me. Barbis is one of those traditional Slovenian names and when Bill made his pitch on the radio, lots of people sat up and took notice.

George Carson didn't work that hard on the Slovenian vote because he assumed that he had it in the bag. That little radio spot featuring Bill Barbis played over and over again on Tony Petkovsek's radio show and this made all the difference in the world.

When the Mayor's race of 1987 came along, I knew I had my work cut out for me when it came to Slovenian-Americans. Mayor Giunta had already established strong ties to the Slovenian National Home and I knew that Tony Petkovsek had already made him his choice. In addition, former Mayor Tony Sustarsic, Slovenian himself, was pushing for the re-election of his successor in this tight-knit community.

But it was about halfway through the campaign that I discovered my secret weapon.

My voice.

You see, the element common to all of the events at the Slovenian Society Home was the very unique form of music called the Cleveland-style polka. Most of you know what a polka is but the Cleveland-style polka has a special joyful lilt to it with a distinct tempo. The Cleveland-style polka was the central focus of Tony Petkovsek's radio program and was the centerpiece of the almost 75 events scheduled each year at Recher Hall.

One Sunday afternoon in September, I was attending a big polka dance at the Hall. The rules allowed political candidates to be introduced if they were members of the Slovenian Society Home. I had that membership card so I was always permitted up on the bandstand so that I could be identified as a candidate.

A light smattering of polite applause usually greeted me after these introductions. Mayor Giunta was permitted the same courtesy, but generally received a much more enthusiastic greeting from the crowd.

Tony Giunta's advantage in these situations was pretty much impossible to overcome. He was more familiar with these folks than I was. The rules of the house, while permitting the introduction of candidates, also prohibited candidates from speaking to the crowd from the stage. How could I turn people into Lynch supporters at these many important ethnic gatherings if I wasn't even allowed to address the crowd to let them know something about me?

Despite these limitations, I continued to show up at these well attended functions, hoping my mere presence and these introductions by the bandleader would chip away at what seemed to be a strong base of support for the formidable incumbent.

It was on that one Sunday afternoon in September at Recher Hall that something special happened. After the standard introduction followed by a smattering of applause, the bandleader made a wisecrack to the crowd: "Too bad Lynch can't sing a polka for us. That might improve his chances."

Everybody laughed.

I shot back a retort loud enough for the bandleader and the entire crowd to hear.

"I could if you'd just give me a chance!"

This brought even more laughter and calls from the crowd to call my bluff. Members of the audience urged the bandleader to put me up on the bandstand in front of the microphone to see if I'd be willing to make a fool of myself.

Rule number one for musicians playing at a dance is to give the crowd what they want. I was ushered up the stairs at the side of the stage and slowly made my way to stand behind the microphone dead center front.

The 1100 people in that room prepared to have a good time at my expense. Aspiring politicians singing in public is almost always a bad idea. Screwing up a polka song at the Slovenian Society Home in Euclid was a sure way to permanently kill off a political career.

But I knew something that no one else in that room knew. I had always been somewhat of a musician and had even been accepted at the Cincinnati Conservatory of Music while a senior in high school. I chose a different path, attending a liberal arts college and then moving on to law school.

While in law school, though, I earned extra money as the lead singer for a 1940s style swing band playing lots of important political functions in Washington, D.C. I worked hard to develop my singing skills and began to make a name for myself as the star male vocalist with the Vic Simas Orchestra.

I was even more fortunate to have a very popular polka in my repertoire. As I faced the people at the Slovenian American home waiting for me to fall flat on my face, the lead saxophonist laughed as he told me that they could play any polka song in any key.

All I had to do was ask. The rest of the guys in the band thought this was hilarious. This Lynch guy was in way over his head.

I smiled and asked him to play the Beer Barrel Polka in the key of E-flat. The faces of the musicians became serious as they flipped through their books for the music in the requested key.

The band started playing the standard introduction to the song. This one was right in my wheelhouse. I hit the notes strong and clear in my second tenor voice.

Those in the audience were stunned. The ladies working in the kitchen left their posts to come out to see who possessed that voice. Folks began to clap their hands, and more importantly, and this is what always happens when a polka is well performed, people began to dance. Dancing a polka involves lots of spinning around in a circle with your partner and as I hit my stride in the rousing chorus of the tune, scores of couples were jumping and spinning throughout the hall like so many tops on the dance floor.

I finished with a high note at the end of the song that was so good people were convinced that a professional singer was running for Mayor of Euclid. The room exploded with cheers and applause.

The crowd asked for more, but I didn't want to ruin the moment. I left the stage without making a speech, complete strangers shaking my hand and patting my back as I worked the crowd looking for votes. That day, I became somewhat of a celebrity in that room full of Slovenian-Americans.

As the campaign wore on, I continued to go to the Slovenian events.

But after that Sunday in September where my singing voice was unveiled, I was always asked to sing a song with whatever polka band was playing that day. Word had gotten out and the Slovenians were curious about this Irish kid who could pull off a good polka with the best of them.

I was happy to satisfy this curiosity. This gave me credibility with the Slovenians that continued to grow as I was repeatedly pushed up to the microphone whenever I attended these Slovenian functions. I left these gatherings feeling uplifted and optimistic about my chances with these very important voters.

On a Friday night in the middle of October, the planets were aligned perfectly for me to luck into a dream opportunity.

Recher Hall that night featured the Godfather of everything polka. In fact, he was known as The Polka King. His name was Frankie Yankovic and Slovenian-Americans practically genuflected at the mere mention of his name.

Yankovic was an international figure whose polkas were so popular that he was awarded a Grammy twice. It was quite a sight when Stevie Wonder and Frankie Yankovic rubbed elbows on national television during the recording industry's annual salute to their highest achievers. Yankovic became so big that Johnny Carson featured him as a guest one night on the Tonight Show.

Yankovic had established his musical career in Northeast Ohio and actually lived in Euclid in 1987. He was to the Polka crowd what Babe Ruth was to baseball fans.

Yankovic's hit songs were popular even in China. They always had a bouncy tune and a hilarious lyric, often politically incorrect. But that's what made them charming in that inimitable Yankovic way.

Yankovic's gigantic smash "She's Too Fat For Me" had an insulting and offensive message but you couldn't help laughing and then grabbing the nearest girl for a twirl across the dance floor when Frankie Yankovic and the Yanks began to play that song.

I couldn't believe my good fortune when Frankie Yankovic called me to the bandstand and asked me to sing a duet with him at that big dinner event in October at Recher hall. I guess he heard that I had some chops.

To make matters even better, we sang one of his legendary numbers called "Cleveland: The Polka Town". It was a real thrill for me apart from the political implications. Singing with The Polka King would be a dream come true for any singer.

And to top it all off, Yankovic winked at me and when we got to the chorus, we changed the refrain to "*Euclid* The Polka Town." Wow! It was the equivalent of getting an endorsement from Elvis! I later found out from my Dad that John Kennedy Lynch the tax lawyer had gotten Yankovic out of a real jam with the IRS a few years earlier. Frankie recognized me as the son of his favorite barrister.

Frankie Yankovic, The Polka King, was an international celebrity.
He made the polka cool long before Weird Al Yankovic came along.
He asked me to join him on stage and it was a big boost for my political career.

Whatever the reason, The Polka King personally advanced my political career with that unbelievable moment on the bandstand that night.

I was elated. I had stumbled upon this musical way to cut into Giunta's support in the Slovenian community.

At the end of the day, as optimistic as I was, I asked myself if putting my singing talents on display at the Slovenian Society Home would actually equate to victory at the polls. After all, the citizens were about to elect a municipal leader, not a musical leader.

I was unsure.

I was singing their song.

But would they be singing mine on November 3?

CHAPTER THIRTY-THREE

Debate

ABOUT TWO WEEKS before the election, a huge candidate forum was held at Euclid High School.

Euclid High School is an imposing building, the only high school in the city. The monstrous structure was built in 1949, with several additions added over the decades to accommodate the city's expanding population.

Although equipped with a beautiful auditorium, the largest room in the complex by far is a large multi-purpose room that can easily accommodate 2,000 people at one time.

This area was more commonly known as the E-room. It was famous as the place where rallies for the high school's basketball, baseball, and football teams were held. Euclid High's enviable record for athletic achievement could be traced in part to the fervor for the sports teams ginned up in these high energy E-room rallies.

I arrived in the E-room to little fanfare twenty minutes before start time.

Tony waited to make his dramatic entrance 15 minutes later. The large throng of Tony's supporters rose to their feet to give their leader a rousing welcome. Tony strolled in, waiving like Charles de Gaulle in his triumphant return to Paris after the defeat of the Germans.

The only thing missing from the scene were little children throwing rose petals before his path on his way up the main aisle and onto the platform erected for the candidates.

I waited nervously for Tony to take his seat and for the mayoral debate to begin. My supporters consisted of my family, friends, some firefighters, and a few policemen, a total of about 90 people.

Tony's supporters numbered about 650, with another 500 or so truly neutral who came to measure the candidate presentations.

The candidate forum was sponsored by the Euclid chapter of the League of Women Voters. The night began with a presentation by each candidate for City Council followed by questions from the audience. The main event, as expected, was the mayoral portion of the debate.

Both Tony and I were given ten minutes for an opening statement followed by one hour of questions from the audience.

The audience wrote questions on index cards and handed them up to the front where the moderator would randomly pull cards from the stack. The question would then be read aloud by an assigned League member and answered by the candidate to whom it was directed. If the question was directed to just one candidate, only the intended target of the question would respond.

As I mentioned, my supporters were outnumbered about 7 to 1. This meant that the vast majority of questions in the stack came from Tony's fans. Would seem like Tony's night, right?

A funny thing happened.

All of Tony's supporters had the same idea. They must have been coached by Frank Chukayne.

All the Coalition supporters who filled out index cards were instructed to dream up some kind of question critical of me to be directed to me. It was obviously Chukayne's theory that he could set me back on my heels by putting me on the hot seat with one question after another identifying my flaws. The Coalition hoped for a public flogging of Lynch.

Sounds like a recipe for disaster, right?

One accusatory question after another fired at me, right?

That's not what happened.

You see, by directing every question to me, the Coalitionists guaranteed that I would have 90% of the microphone time during the question-and-answer period. If the League of Women Voters had designed the format to permit both candidates to answer each question, Tony would've had equal time. But the rules required that the responses come only from those to whom the tough inquiries were directed. As a result, I had ample time to make my case.

Every time a question was aimed at me, as almost all of them were, I turned the question around. I redirected the question and showed how the attack on me reflected on Tony Giunta as the true offender.

If the question criticized my lack of experience in financial management, I described Tony's extravagant overspending habits.

If the question attacked me for supporting fair housing, I went after Tony's loathsome creation of ghetto conditions at the Euclid Housing project.

If the question said that I couldn't be counted on to keep Euclid safe, I pointed to Tony's underfunding the police and fire departments.

By the time the night ended, Tony's supporters were angry and frustrated. Tony wanted to jump in as my answers became a severe criticism of his leadership.

At one point, the moderator told Tony's cheering section to shut up. She told them that if they thought the Q & A session was unfair to Tony, they should not have directed so many of their index cards to me.

The reigning champion was left defenseless while I pummeled away at his midsection. Incredibly, this also resulted in a surprisingly good write-up in the local newspaper. More importantly, the few hundred folks that were uncommitted before they arrived at the hall came away with a revelation: this kid had confidence and poise.

Maybe he could handle the mayor's job.

At least I got people talking.

CHAPTER THIRTY-FOUR

I Want to be Left a Lawn

ONE OF THE KEYS TO SUCCESS in local municipal elections in the late 1980's was the use of lawn signs.

This was especially true in Euclid, because the major thoroughfares are dotted with homes where front yards constitute prime real estate in establishing name recognition.

The Coalition had a magnificent list of lawn sign locations in its arsenal because hundreds of city workers would place lawn signs for Tony Giunta on their own front lawns and they could also use the front yards of their many relatives.

This meant that overnight, the Coalition could plant 1500 lawn signs throughout the city in key locations so that motorists couldn't help but notice the strength of the Coalition base. This was pretty intimidating for candidates trying to compete against City Hall politicos.

Actually obtaining permission from a homeowner to place a political yard sign was difficult and time-consuming as well.

In addition, many people who supported the idea of bringing the Coalition's reign to an end did not want to make their political position known. Publicly opposing Tony could have consequences. Mark Jochum used to have an answer for those discouraged by the Coalition's lawn sign muscle: lawn signs don't vote, people do.

Despite the automatic advantage the Coalition always seemed to have in the lawn sign department, Nancy and I decided to spend a lot of our resources on this seemingly rudimentary campaign technique.

Our thinking was that if we could somehow offer the Coalition some competition in this area, it would create the impression that David Lynch was a credible candidate.

We did not think that we could match Tony sign for sign. But we did think the placement of a few hundred signs might convince voters that Lynch was more than just your normal cannon fodder to be blasted away by the Coalition howitzers.

Many of the sign locations resulted from my conversations with citizens on their doorsteps. Occasionally, some brave soul would consent to the placement of our Lynch for Mayor lawn sign that featured white cardboard and bright blue lettering.

The lawn signs also presented a couple of practical challenges. In 1987 lawn sign technology was unsophisticated. Political lawn signs today consist of sleek wire frames with a plastic baggie-style sign stretched over the frame to allow the candidate's name to be seen on both sides.

Back in 1987, a political lawn sign was made from a wooden frame nailed together, with the cardboard sign stapled to the frame. This is much more expensive than the modern design. Installation of the sign was also difficult because it required hammering the wooden stakes of the frame into the soil already becoming hard with the approach of winter.

Nothing is as miserable as standing in front of someone's house on a cold blustery night hammering a sign into the ground and watching the staples pull loose, the cardboard surface blowing away down the street.

The theft of lawn signs was also problematic. The Coalition used to go around town in the middle of the night, throwing my signs into the back of a pickup truck, the signs usually ending up in a dumpster behind a shopping center, always broken and destroyed.

I can remember filing a police report over this lawn sign mischief. It really was a crime of theft. The desk sergeant over at the police station used to laugh over these reports because the police chief considered the Coalition's theft of my signs effective political strategy. All is fair in love and war, he used to say. It troubled me that Chief Frank Payne considered the Coalition sign vandalism and theft to be a form of legitimate politicking.

We told our own people not to touch the Coalition signs. It's not that we were particularly noble. We assumed that theft of Fat Tony's signs would land somebody in jail after an appearance in front of Stick'em Niccum.

In the war of the lawn signs, however, the Coalition had created an opportunity for us. It was the element of surprise. You see, the Coalition councilmen had just a few years earlier passed an ordinance that prohibited the placement of political lawn signs until after October 15 preceding the November election.

They wanted to minimize the time period for political lawn signs trashing the appearance of the beautiful residential neighborhoods in Euclid. This proved to be an advantage for the Lynch campaign.

We worked very hard to obtain sign locations.

The Coalition was caught off guard when about 800 lawn signs urging my election seemed to spontaneously sprout up in the neighborhoods during the middle of October.

Of course, the Coalition placed their standard 1500 signs as they had done for years and we were outnumbered.

But then something remarkable happened during the last three weeks of the campaign. The firefighters and the police began to make phone calls. Sign locations were presented to Nancy and by October 21, we had just as many lawn sign locations as the Coalition.

Then something even more fantastic occurred. Our 1500 lawn sign locations started some kind of chain reaction with our supporters. Suddenly, folks realized that a Lynch lawn sign wasn't something to be afraid of. More requests for lawn signs poured in almost to the point where we couldn't keep up with them. My brother-in-law, a carpenter by trade, was in our garage every night building frames while the rest of my family stapled the blue-and-white cardboard to the frames.

Nancy was like a field general, deploying every person she could think of to go out into the night with a trunk full of lawn signs, placing new ones as the requests came in and just as importantly, replacing signs that had been stolen or damaged.

I hate to think the trees we killed with all the wood and cardboard consumed in this effort. By the time election day rolled around, the Lynch campaign had achieved somewhat of a lawn sign miracle.

We had a total of over 3500 lawn sign locations throughout the city. People knew who we were and they knew that this challenge to the Coalition's dominance was real.

We also knew that the Giunta for Mayor Committee remained confident. They had history on their side. If they were worried, they sure did not show it.

Political experts noticed the Lynch lawn signs, but declared this to be a minor anomaly. As we moved closer to election day itself, the pundits weighed in and predicted that Lynch would be vanquished like every other candidate that had opposed a Coalition Mayor.

Despite that, the lawn signs made us feel good about the campaign because it gave us a sense that we were not alone. Inside each one of those homes, somebody was thinking that Lynch might make a good mayor.

City of Euclid Building Commissioner Bill Carney turned out to be somewhat of a silent hero when it came to the battle of the lawn signs. You see, the City Council passed an ordinance requiring candidates to submit a list of lawn sign locations to the Building Commissioner. This was sheer political intimidation, designed to make it easy for Coalition operatives to identify the opponent's supporters. Imagine Giunta, armed with that list, making calls to complain about the presence of a Lynch sign on your front lawn.

Carney, to his credit, smelled a rat when Chukayne called to get a copy of the Lynch locations. I don't know how he got away with it, but Carney, a longtime Coalitionist, pretended to experience technical problems in maintaining the list of Lynch locations. We were getting help from high places.

We would need a lot more help along the way but we were beginning to feel like we just might have a chance. Every time we drove the streets of Euclid and saw those white and blue signs, we felt better about things.

We were beginning to experience a feeling foreign to us up until this point: optimism.

CHAPTER THIRTY-FIVE

The Last Hurrah

THE CITY felt so alive in last days of October preceding the election.

The lethargy of the warm summer was gone and the crisp cool air of Northeast Ohio quickened the pace of my assault on the front and side doors of unsuspecting residents. By this time, I had only about 400 homes left to visit before election day.

Piece of cake.

There was one more big prize available before the election itself and I coveted that prize.

The endorsement from the *Euclid News Journal* newspaper.

Endorsements were virtually nonexistent for me during this campaign. The two daily newspapers, *The Plain Dealer* and *The News-Herald*, had already endorsed Tony Giunta.

In addition, every sitting government official within one hundred miles, apart from Farrell and Jochum, had endorsed Giunta. Absolutely nobody of note thought I had any chance at all. It was frustrating and depressing.

Our campaign team laughed because we had received one lonely endorsement: the local Sierra Club. This occurred because I opposed the opening of a nuclear power plant in Perry, Ohio about 50 miles east of Euclid. Unfortunately, Euclidians in 1987 really didn't care about the Sierra Club. Meanwhile, Giunta's literature didn't have enough space to list all his endorsements.

However, we felt that we could overcome this embarrassing lack of public endorsements. That's because we believed one crucial endorsement remained and we sensed it was within reach.

The *Euclid News Journal* covered only one city: Euclid.

Like a blanket.

Their reporters attended every meeting of City Council, the zoning board, and school board. Generally speaking, they were objective. They editorialized only occasionally with a mild critique of Coalition policy.

That's because like Chicago during the old Mayor Daley years, the trains ran on time. Euclid was, after all, a great place to live and raise a family.

If you were white.

And the *Euclid News Journal* was an important vehicle for local information. Everyone read this weekly newspaper published on Thursdays.

Everyone. If you wanted, you could go to the late-night store on Wednesdays and find Thursday morning's paper on the newsstands.

The Coalition counted on the paper publishing news of projects coming out of City Hall. Fat Tony and Pat Rocco could get a *News Journal* reporter to come to City Hall for an interview at the drop of a hat.

It was a symbiotic relationship. The newspaper needed news and City Hall wanted the PR.

Of course, this could make for some pretty unexciting reading. That's why the trio of Joe Farrell, Mark Jochum, and David Lynch had a role to play. As the paper reported the stupendous achievements of the Coalition, the vocal minority was Side B of this familiar record.

The paper had developed a common theme for all their stories. Coalition: the big mo' rolls on. Three Amigos: proceed with caution.

A typical story involved 13 paragraphs about a new ball diamond added to the city's spectacular recreation facilities followed by two paragraphs quoting Mark Jochum's concern about the financing of the project.

That's why I studied like a madman so I could be prepared for the *News Journal* endorsement interview. This could be a magical opportunity. The *News Journal* endorsement was important. Bigger than any other. The *News Journal* in those days was the paper of record. The interview was scheduled for two weeks before the election and both candidates would be questioned simultaneously.

Tony versus me.

The Coalition Mayor would have to face me at the newspaper offices without Rocco or Chukayne or Oyaski to help him. Tony was a big picture guy who left details to staff. I knew that if I could get Tony bogged down in complex issues like municipal financing and economic development, I could blow him out of the water.

That's exactly what happened.

Asked about incentives for industry, I came armed with a detailed knowledge of federal, state, and county assistance programs. Tony was at a loss for words as the editors pressed him for details.

To his credit, Tony pointed to the record over the many years that the Coalition guided the good ship Euclid.

The journalists wouldn't let him off the hook. They wanted specific plans and all Tony could do was tell them that a great city remains great when successful leadership continues in office. I had a plan for the wastewater treatment plant, police jail, employee health insurance, and reorganization of the Parks and Recreation department. I even had a plan to reduce the cost of trash pickup in the city.

It was a triumph!

I left the interview feeling like a conquering hero. The only thing missing was a ticker tape parade as I drove home. Nancy was as excited as I was when I gave her a report of the meeting.

Word circulated throughout our campaign and the tension began to build. We were filled with anticipation as the newspaper endorsement was expected to be published on the Thursday preceding election Tuesday.

As was my habit, I got hold of the crucial edition on Wednesday night. I brought the paper home but couldn't bear to look until I got home so that Nancy and I could open it up together. This could be just the thing we needed to make it a race. The *News Journal* endorsement was everything in this town. We nervously flipped to the opinion page.

"The Last Hurrah"

That was the name of the editorial recommending voters return Tony Giunta to City Hall.

I was crestfallen. Destroyed.

Incredulous.

Impossible!

There it was in black and white.

Vote for Tony.

Here was their logic, if you can call it that.

Lynch was smart and knowledgeable and talented. But he wasn't quite ready. Go with the old hand. Don't take chances with an untried commodity when Tony has gas left in the tank.

Tony deserves another chance. He may not be brilliant but he is experienced and steady. Give him another term.

A last hurrah.

It was peculiar that the editors captioned the endorsement "The Last Hurrah". The title was borrowed from Edwin O'Connor's bestselling 1956 book of the same name about a crooked big city boss. The novel loosely paralleled the career of Boston Mayor James Curley who was known for ruthless campaigns and questionable ethics.

Spencer Tracy's portrayal of Mayor Curley in the 1958 film version won him the best actor award from the National Board of Review.

Movie veteran John Ford took the honors for best director. It's a terrific movie.

"The Last Hurrah" was an award-winning film and the title of the Sun Journal's endorsement of Mayor Giunta.

But this was bizarre. The newspaper's endorsement article was named after a novel about a crooked mayor and it recommended that Euclidians vote for the man I viewed as a crooked mayor. Man, that smarted.

I was so close.

But with a thud, my candidacy hit the mat at the hands of what felt like a knockout blow delivered by this hometown periodical.

Too late to quit.

Keep going. Just a few days left.

Hold your head high.

And pray for a miracle.

The Party Center

THE DAY BEFORE THE ELECTION, I visited the Apollo party center. I had reserved the big banquet hall as my victory center election night. As I approached the Apollo, I saw a big lime-green notice glued to the front door. "Closed by order of the City of Euclid Building Department."

What?

In 24 hours, I needed to be in that building with my supporters swilling beers and celebrating the end of a long campaign. Had the Apollo been a victim of Coalition vindictiveness?

Was it a sin to rent to the candidate running against Fat Tony? Was it a violation of the building code to do so?

Probably not.

But here in Euclid, anything was possible. I was suspicious. Calls to the party center's management went unanswered.

I scrambled to find a substitute location. I had few takers. By now everyone in town knew my name and I was a marked man. The poor fellow who is trying to unseat Tony.

Phone calls to find a last-minute gathering place for election night had a theme to them.

They would go something like this.

"Sure, I'd love to help. What's your name again? Lynch? You the guy who's running for Mayor? Oh yeah, well, we're booked Tuesday night. Sorry."

Really? I mean, Tuesdays aren't exactly a big party night in Euclid.

Finally, I found one brave businessman.

Ivan Kuhar.

He had just purchased a landmark bar in Euclid called Tracy's Tavern. It had been a place for generously poured drinks and solid food for many years. The Friday night fish fries were legendary.

Ivan had a thick accent. He was first-generation Slovenian, despite the Russian first name. He had rechristened Tracy's as Kuhar's. He had no use for the City Hall crowd and welcomed my business. He had a small party room off the main bar. It was mine for the asking and all I had to do was pay for the beer consumed. No problem.

By the time the building department would learn of this rental, the election would be over. All we had to do was keep the location secret until the polls closed Tuesday night. We would make a few phone calls on election day and ask our people to congregate.

Ivan was hosting the rebels.

I hoped he was hosting history.

CHAPTER THIRTY-SEVEN

The Night Before

THE MONDAY NIGHT before the election there was a regularly scheduled meeting of the Euclid City Council. I didn't know what fate had in store for me the next day but I felt compelled to do my duty this one last time before I faced the voters.

So I attended the meeting and took my seat with my colleagues on our city's legislative body.

Giunta, Rocco, and Chukayne sat across from me, staring at me throughout the meeting. I guess they thought they could mow me down with their gaze. I ignored them.

I don't remember much of the council debate that night. I could think of little else other than what the last ten months of my life had been dedicated to: ending the Coalition era. When the Council President hit the gavel marking the close of the meeting, I was exhausted and excited all at the same time.

Joe Farrell came up to me to wish me luck and shake my hand. He told me to stand proud regardless of the outcome in 24 hours.

He hugged me. "You are loved by God."

The room emptied quickly except for Giunta pausing to ask Pat Boyce for a word. Boyce had been in attendance in case the council took action related to the firefighters' union contract. They didn't. Giunta pulled the legislation from the agenda right there at the meeting.

The Mayor wanted to wait until after the election. The Mayor felt that his impending re-election victory would give him just a bit more leverage against the union, allowing him to change the contract in his favor.

Giunta walked up to Boyce and firmly ordered him to report to the Mayor's office at nine o'clock on Wednesday morning after election Tuesday.

"I'm going to teach you firefighters what real hardball politics is all about!"

Boyce smiled calmly and promised that he would be obedient and present himself at City Hall Wednesday morning.

I was the last to leave the council chambers.

By myself in that room where so much history had been made, I paused. The chambers began to go dark as the janitor turned off the lights. Illumination slipped away as the light switches were shifted into the off position one at a time.

This was the place, I thought to myself, where Ken Sims struggled mightily to make government noble. Mayor Sims dedicated these same council chambers in 1938 with these words: "May these walls never be soiled with political trickery or corruption."

Sims passed away in 1975. But his ideal of honest responsive government wasn't dead. It's just that his beloved Coalition was no longer the keeper of that flame. Had it been passed on to me?

Now in total darkness, I said a silent prayer.

Then I went home.

Election Day

NOVEMBER 3, 1987. The election had finally arrived.

My family and friends had been pressed into service for the day. We wanted to be certain that every single polling location had someone standing on site to promote my candidacy at each of the 29 locations. Not so easy when you consider that the polls opened at 6:30 AM and closed at 7:30 PM.

13 hours!

I was up at around 4 AM.

As the day dawned, I was running on fumes.

The entire campaign, seemingly my entire life, all boiled down to this day.

The weather was gray, overcast, with a slight drizzle of rain. The temperature was about 39 degrees Fahrenheit. Our game plan was to have others cover the polling stations on my behalf. I was then free to roam the city, moving from one place to another, depending on reports of heavy voter turnout at various spots.

It was a good strategy because for no particular reason, flash crowds of voters would materialize at certain locations. The library would be heavy for an hour and then I'd high tail it over to the high school because of big crowds.

Nancy and I were exhausted but the act of greeting voters seemed to energize us.

It felt relatively positive, but it's always hard to tell. Voters are generally polite but a smile and a handshake are hardly an effective exit poll.

Every now and then, a voter returning to the parking lot would give me a thumbs-up sign to confirm having voted for me. The most common voter response, however, was that of staring straight ahead, refusing any offered literature, and marching in to do their duty.

Nancy and I at the voting booth on election day: I pretended to be uncertain.

It was pretty clear most voters really see casting a ballot as a private act. They just want to be left alone. For this reason, I recognized when to back off as the voter was arriving.

Some folks would be insulted that I wanted to campaign just as they entered the polling place. I knew that I would begin to lose votes if I even tried to greet those who wanted me to give them their space.

So I tried to be careful that day. Ohio law requires campaigners to remain 100 feet away from the polling place, so the building is ringed by a politics-free zone on election day.

However, there were quite a few voters who were thrilled to see the actual candidate in the flesh. These citizens were warm and friendly, so I thanked them for voting, shook their hand, and asked them to think of me when they cast their ballot. Short, simple, sincere.

I felt pretty good when I got home that night. I'd been reasonably well received by voters at the polling places as I stood outside. I was upbeat.

Another piece of good news was our discovery that the Board of Elections had developed a punch card voting system where the punch cards could be read only by machines located at the Board's headquarters in downtown Cleveland. This meant that for this election, the Coalition poll workers in Euclid were stripped of the power and authority to count the vote. They couldn't even if they wanted to.

Automated reading of punch cards downtown eliminated polling place vote counting. I was going to get an honest count!

Tired at the end of this long day, I called the Board of Elections. It was 7:50 PM and the polls had been closed for 20 minutes.

Of course, it took hours to count the tallies. However, absentee votes had arrived at the Board of Elections several days before the election itself. With the polls closed, the board was permitted to release these absentee vote totals.

I couldn't believe it when the clerk on the other end of the phone told me the percentages based on the absentee vote.

Giunta 65%.

Lynch 35%.

In Euclid, the absentee voters were senior citizens too frail to make it to the polls. Today, you don't even need a reason to vote absentee. But in 1987, you had to have an excuse based on physical condition or being out of town. In addition, the absentee results generally mirrored the outcome for the older citizens across the board. Seniors also represented those most likely to vote. The younger the age, the less likely the citizen will even make the effort to vote. Those were the stats back then.

Let me spell it out for you.

It was the wisdom of the day that losing the absentees was tantamount to losing the election.

I was sick.

65% to 35%!

How do you describe the feeling of crash and burn when you are the unfortunate pilot?

I prefer showers to baths, but at that point I felt like I could barely stand on my feet.

The time. The effort.

The money. The humiliation.

What was I thinking?

I stepped into a hot tub, sat down, and soaked.

And sulked.

Nancy told me to keep my chin up.

I continued to soak in that tub.

Our victory party (ha!) was scheduled for Kuhar's party room at 9 PM. Nancy told me to get out of the tub and get dressed.

Did I really want to attend this wake? Wouldn't my supporters rather go home and get some sleep?

Tears and blame awaited me and I didn't want to go. Nancy said that not going would be classless. She was right.

So I got dressed and went.

CHAPTER THIRTY-NINE

How it Ended

ABOUT THIRTY PEOPLE were milling about when I arrived at the modest party room in the back of Kuhar's.

Nancy started calling downtown for more vote updates. It was the only way to get information as online results were not in place in 1987. It was also a relatively slow process because voting was done by punch cards for that election.

The Board of Elections had only so many machines to read the cards. They fed the cards into machines in batches. Every 20 minutes or so, a new batch was counted and we moved a little closer to knowing the final results.

That demoralizing 65% to 35% absentee result was all we had until about 9:30 PM. At 9:32, Nancy got the first batch of non-absentee results.

Giunta's lead had tapered only slightly. Giunta 64%, Lynch 36%.

Oh well.

I mean, how do you win a football game when you're behind by seven touchdowns in the first quarter? The somber quiet of that room gave me a chance to thank each volunteer personally. These were my comrades in arms in the political foxholes and I cherished their dedication.

They too had hopes of ending the Coalition stranglehold on local government. I was their hope. Unfortunately, I was taking a beating.

9:57 PM: Giunta 62%, Lynch, 38%.

At least I wasn't completely destroyed. I took some comfort in the fact that the tally was sliding toward a more respectable defeat.

Meanwhile, the Coalition had set up their victory party at the East Side Irish American Club. This was the largest venue in the City of Euclid, capable of holding about ten Kuhar's Taverns. It was typical for fifteen hundred souls to gather on election night to support the Coalition, and tonight was no exception.

It was ironic that one of Ohio's most popular Italians enjoyed the accommodations at the Irish Club that night while the only Irishman in the race was crammed into the tiny backroom at a Slovenian bar.

Those who were gathered at Tony's celebration describe the crowd as happy but a little bored. The Coalition always won so Tony's substantial lead was nothing special. It was kind of like an Ohio State football game where the Buckeyes are playing some division three school. The powerful are expected to vanquish the weak, so it was difficult to become energized about the Mayor's re-election. 10:19 PM: Giunta 59%, Lynch 41%.

Rocco chews on the ever-present cigar, accepting congratulations from well-wishers. He had masterminded another Coalition sweep. All the Coalition councilmen were being returned to office and Tony seemed to have things well in hand.

Rocco would not begin to celebrate, however. He wanted an ironclad confirmation. He knew that there were many votes left to be counted and he didn't like the trend. He was concerned that a long night ahead remained.

Giunta called him a worry wart. "This one is over," Tony told him.

The Mayor left Rocco to his reverie in a side office at the Irish Club and joined the festive crowd in their enjoyment of the Polka band hired to add to the fun. Everyone was patting him on the back and shaking his hand. Everybody wanted a piece of the winner.

The band played "Happy Days Are Here Again."

The crowd at the Irish Club actually began to dissipate. Ho-hum, Tony wins again. Let's go home now because I have to work tomorrow.

10:26 PM and it was Giunta 57% and Lynch 43%. Giunta scribbled some notes on a napkin and prepared to address the loyalists growing impatient waiting for him to deliver his victory speech. Giunta told Rocco to join him on the bandstand.

Rocco stopped him. Wait. He told him to wait. Giunta laughed at him, calling him a wet blanket. Rocco looked at Giunta and raised his voice.

"I said wait!"

10:39 PM and the election board reported Giunta 55% and Lynch 45%.

Back at Lynch headquarters, a slight buzz began in the room. The tally was moving in the direction of something interesting. The group of 30 people expanded to about 75 folks gathered for some beer and fun.

10:56 PM: Giunta 53%, Lynch 47%.

Could it be?

The crowd was now a mob.

Two hundred people were crammed into Mr. Kuhar's tiny room that had a fire marshal limit of 150. The atmosphere was no longer a buzz. It was more like the roar of a jet engine. As Nancy announced each new total, the excitement and the tension grew even more.

We couldn't believe the events unfolding before us.

I tried to remain calm amid the chaos and the din.

It was the feeling that a jockey must have when riding a horse that finds a burst of pure speed that you hope is good enough to win.

If there's enough track left to catch the leader. For us, enough track meant enough votes remaining for the trend to continue.

Were there enough votes left to edge out the incumbent?

Impossible.

But…

The next update was announced by Nancy at 11:32 PM.

Giunta 52%, Lynch 48%. By now, upwards of 500 people formed a carpet of humanity at the party center.

Mr. Kuhar was running out of beer.

Talking was impossible.

You had to yell to be heard.

C'mon, Bessie, move your keister! You can do it!

These folks had bet on a long shot, and they prayed their horse could squeak it out.

Word was out. Something special was developing at the Lynch for Mayor gathering. Non-supporters came to the hall just in case something historic happened.

The wait for the next batch of votes seemed to take an eternity.

We were told that the last group of votes remained to be counted.

They arrived at 11:47.

Nancy announced Giunta 51%, Lynch 49%.

For about ten seconds, the room went silent as the idea that I had lost by a narrow margin seemed apparent. Someone handed Nancy a note. The board had misinformed her. One additional batch of votes remained to be counted in those machines reading the punch cards downtown. Nancy told everyone to wait. Someone from the back complained that they couldn't hear her.

She raised her voice.

"I said wait!"

We couldn't breathe.

I know people were talking to me, but I wasn't processing. I was in the final throes of a heavyweight fight and I was barely standing, figuratively speaking.

Nancy and I looked at each other every now and then. With our eyes, we said to each other "Holy Crap!"

At 12:01 AM., Nancy got the final from the board of elections.

She told me nothing but approached the microphone dialed up to the max so that she could be heard in the noisy room.

She insisted on quiet. That took a minute to achieve given the raucous group. She had been announcing the results all night long by giving Tony Giunta's totals first.

In addition, she had been begun each announcement of the vote totals with the words "Mayor Giunta" has so-and-so percent.

This time, she began "Mister Giunta" and I knew Tony was king no more.

Mr. Giunta 48%, Lynch 52%!

The explosive blast from the sea of supporters was something I'll never forget as long as I live. Someone threw open the doors of the hall. We heard the blare of sirens and saw the flashing of red and white lights. The firefighters of Euclid were driving the hook and ladder trucks up and down the streets of the City of Euclid in celebration.

The scene was wild beyond belief.

Nobody who was there forgot what happened that night.

Over at the Irish-American club, Mayor Giunta's wife fainted, out cold over the shock of the final outcome. Someone called 911 but Mayor Giunta told his friends that he wanted to drive his wife to the local hospital himself. He didn't want to go in a City of Euclid ambulance likely to be driven by a member of the City Fire department. Only moments after the election's conclusion, he was already blaming the fire union. His anger outweighed the need for professional help in transporting his bride. The former first lady of Euclid recovered and went home that same night.

Rocco disappeared. No one knew where he had gone but somehow he had slipped away. The man who was a master of words couldn't figure out what to say so he just went away.

He was in a state of complete shock, emotionally and deep down into the core of his soul. After fifty years of ruling the waves, the mighty steamship Coalition had run aground with his hand on the rudder.

Rocco would never recover. His friends reported his spirit broken, those close to him saying he occasionally gets a vacant look in his eyes and admits that he overreached.

David Jones, the Godfather of political writers in Northeast Ohio, wrote in the News-Herald that this was the biggest political upset in the history of Cuyahoga County.

I cannot adequately describe the insanity of the evening's conclusion. Everybody at Kuhar's felt like they had just won the World Series and the Super Bowl all at the same time.

Moments after the final tally: bedlam!

The Beatles escorted into Shea stadium saw the mania as crowds essentially lost control with delirious joy. That's what Nancy and I experienced as the impenetrable fortress of the Coalition came tumbling down that night as the final vote tally was read. It was improbable.

It was impossible.

Yet it was true. And this has been the story of how it happened.

Little David can beat Goliath.

Sometimes you need a slingshot. And sometimes you need to ring doorbells and enlist the help of firefighters and policemen.

And Joe Farrell.

CHAPTER FORTY

Epilogue

PAT BOYCE appeared at Mayor Giunta's office at nine o'clock the next morning as instructed. The secretary sent him away. She told him it wasn't a good time.

I attempted to set up a transition with the outgoing administration. Nothing doing. Mayor Giunta wouldn't return any of my calls.

He held a press conference accusing me of conducting a dirty campaign, highlighting my reference to his family in criticizing the city payroll. I responded that hiring his family members was unethical and fair game in a local campaign. If you don't want to expose your children, don't put them on the payroll, I declared.

This didn't help matters. Giunta announced his own version of a transition: He would throw me the keys to the building on January 1, 1988. The media's reaction to this was loud and harsh. Tony was going out on a very sour note. None of this helped his legacy but it created a sympathetic environment for me as I tried to figure out what to do next.

Mayor Giunta left me a little present for my first day in office. On December 31, 1987, just hours before I assumed my new role as Mayor, Giunta fired all the directors of each department. An Alberta clipper was about to dump twenty-four inches of snow on our city and the former mayor thought it would be nice to leave me without a service director to face this major weather crisis.

I called Giunta's Service Director John Piscitello just as the crystal ball was dropping at Times Square and informed him that the new mayor was about to make a midnight visit to his home. I handed him a letter reappointing him, letting him know he could prove himself by getting the streets cleared. Grateful for the opportunity, John did a great job deploying an array of plow operators who worked all through the frigid New Year's night with superb results.

I went to the service garage at 3 AM and dished out bowls of steaming hot clam chowder to the weary snow fighters. To Giunta's dismay and chagrin, the City of Euclid remained the "City of Superior Services" under the Lynch administration.

I took the oath of office in the auditorium of the Shore Cultural Center, a former high school building outgrown by the school district decades earlier. Shore was somewhat of a landmark building, many a local hero having graced its hallways, including Mayor Giunta, who graduated from Shore High School. He did not attend the ceremony. I was sworn in by Ralph Locher, Chief Justice of the Ohio Supreme Court, a Democrat and former Mayor of the City of Cleveland.

I was determined to effect change in Euclid, but I also wanted the old-timers to know the sky was not falling. I wanted to project a thoughtful attitude, not making any rash moves. I was going to lead the city as opposed to beating it over the head.

One of my first priorities was injecting modern thinking into the Euclid Police Department. This was going to be tough with the icon Frank Payne running the police as he had for decades.

I decided on day one to drive over to visit the Chief in his office, the famous lair known for its ugly lime-green shag carpet and dark oak paneled walls covered with celebrity photos. Big shots wanted pictures with the world-renowned chief and an extra print always ended up on the chief's wall of fame.

Getting in to see the chief turned out to be a hilarious problem. I had an appointment to see him, but Payne neglected to inform his staff.

I parked right in front of the police headquarters and sauntered in wearing a dark-gray suit and conservative tie. I could feel the sergeant at the window watching me as I strode through the doors. I tried to announce my purpose in being there but the burly desk sergeant cut me off.

"You can't park there, " he informed me.

" Yes, but…"

"No buts. Just move your car."

"You don't understand, I'm here to see …"

Now he was getting angry. " I don't care who you're here to see, son. Just move your vehicle or we will tow it for you! " he threatened.

Behind the desk sergeant, I could see a group of giggling office workers having a good laugh at the sergeant's expense. They recognized me as Euclid's youngest mayor, newly minted for the job. But to Sergeant Kushma, before him was a young man who needed to learn respect for authority.

I made a few more feeble attempts to clarify my position, but to no avail.

What to do? I didn't want to begin my career as mayor with an arrest for disorderly conduct. I did what seemed to be the simplest and obvious thing to do.

I walked out the front door and got into my car to find a place in the visitor's parking lot in the back of the building.

I was just pulling out when the doors of the building flew open with Sergeant Kushma, face beet-red, yelling for me to wait.

I waited. He apologized. He had no idea, he said. I smiled and told him there was nothing wrong with a man doing his job. Heck, I couldn't believe I was the mayor, why should he?

Poor Kushma, he never lived that one down.

In any case, I finally made it into the Chief's inner sanctum.

I began by telling the Chief how the community loved and appreciated him and his over-fifty years of service. I told him, however, that he had earned a glorious retirement, and that it might be time to turn the reins over to a new chief.

Payne smiled and surprised me by saying that he agreed and would seriously consider my suggestion. He shook my hand warmly. I was pleased at this reception, especially since I had presented such a bold idea.

Unfortunately, the chief had a surprise in store for me. I turned on the six o'clock news and there was Payne, announcing he had been fired by the new mayor.

That rat! I hadn't fired him, but merely suggested his retirement, the chief responding in a generally positive fashion. Worst of all, the chief knew that I didn't have the authority to fire him. Euclid's Civil Service law made the chief a tested position, the selection made by the Civil Service Commission.

The gist of the TV story was that a young, brash, inexperienced politician was engaging in age-discrimination, pushing the chief out the door because of his advanced years. I came across as a jerk, despite my explanation to the media.

Luckily, no real showdown would develop. The chief applied for retirement with the state Police Pension Board. At his retirement dinner, the chief admitted that he had been ready to hang up his badge for years, and that he was grateful to me for helping him make that decision.

I wasn't out of the woods yet, though, when it came to the police chief. I now needed a new one to be selected by the Civil Service Commission. Giunta's last days turned out to be the gift that keeps on giving.

On his last day in office, Giunta appointed Rocco the head of the Civil Service Commission. Rumor had it that Payne had already designated his successor, Wayne Baumgart, to carry forward the Coalition style of police work. With Rocco now directing the Civil Service Commission, it seemed likely that Euclid would face another fifty years of Frank Payne reconfigured in a younger version.

The testing went as expected. My preference, Captain Pat Kordet, a veteran of many years, was universally respected, always putting the law above politics. According to Rocco, Kordet finished second to Baumgart in the testing. I sensed something rotten was afoot.

I researched ways to override the Civil Service results to allow me to appoint Kordet. To his credit, Kordet wanted no part of this. Kordet respected Baumgart and told me to give Wayne a chance. He advised that using some legal ruse to circumvent the system would create doubt as to the legitimacy of a Kordet appointment. Baumgart had legitimately prevailed in the testing process, according to Captain Kordet.

I backed off and it was a wise decision. Baumgart, I learned, had cut his teeth as a patrolman in the Cleveland Heights police department. Rumors of his Coalition leanings were wrong, he explained.

Wayne Baumgart: proved to be an outstanding chief.   *Pat Kordet: a man of honor.*

Wayne would prove to be more than up to the task. He provided honest new leadership for the police department. He initiated an ambitious training program for this organization that had become stuck in the 1950's. Chief Baumgart was everything one could hope for. He also modernized police weapons and the radio communications system. Baumgart's advanced training concepts gave Euclid educated police men and women solving problems, not just making arrests.

I am sure this drove Rocco crazy. Baumgart was making me look good through his effective administration of law enforcement. Baumgart even made Kordet his second in command.

Wayne and I became fast friends, he forgiving my Kordet conspiracy, both of us sharing a desire to attain excellence in government service. I also discovered that Wayne possessed a spectacular tenor voice and was a talented guitar player.

This resulted in an entertaining and if I do say so myself, inspiring duet: Wayne and I developed a two-part harmony version of the Star Spangled Banner performed at various events. It must have been quite a sight with the Mayor and the Police chief making like the Everly brothers all over town.

And Wayne did one more thing to show he had good taste: he got rid of the ugly lime green carpet.

Poor Tony never got to move into his beloved new City Hall complex because it was not completed while he was mayor. Unbelievably, I had to finish the structure! I wasn't too happy about that as it turned out that Tony had under-budgeted.

The City council forced me to find the extra money to complete the ill-advised project. Finish it I did, though. My new administration moved into the building, about one year after my election, with little fanfare. It was strange taking residence in the place that I so aggressively opposed.

Truth be told though, the "Giuntadome" had been key to my success on election night. Few missed the irony of it all.

There was some talk around this time of naming the new city hall after Mayor Giunta. After all, some reasoned, Giunta pushed it through despite the political price he ultimately paid. This talk died down however when Giunta's supporters realized that naming the structure after Tony would likely mean the derisive "Giuntadome" name would be associated with the building forever.

After they discovered that Mayor Giunta had decimated the general fund as well, City Council insisted on millions of dollars in operating spending cuts. I was only too happy to accommodate them. Council had inadvertently handed me the ax I needed to cut out the loads of dead wood at city hall.

Sam the barber was among the long list of those who were cut-off from the government trough. The county took over weights and measures. Employees who remained in municipal service worked harder and smarter. Performance levels actually went up. Workers realized that I may have been young but I took efficient use of tax dollars seriously.

Paul Oyaski put the public good above politics and agreed to become my Law Director, creating a much needed rapport between me and the Coalition City Council suddenly without a leader. They were like members of a band without a music director. They didn't know what songs to play. Oyaski helped guide them in a new direction.

This made a huge difference and I was able to pass scores of reforms in the bidding process and in making government more transparent. We changed the charter almost immediately to reverse the Rocco scheme: next in line to become mayor reverted back to the council president. Rocco concluded that Oyaski must have been a spy working for the Lynch campaign all along. Oyaski finally realized his potential by escaping out from under the influence of Rocco and the Coalition.

The Coalition was now finally dead and buried. It was like the collapse of the Berlin Wall because no one would have imagined such a thing just a few years earlier.

Although Louie Paroska passed away in 1993, his daughter Kathy, who was just 17 when I unseated Fat Tony, inherited her father's passion for justice in the political system. Kathy formed a company to assist dynamic political campaigns and today she is one of the most highly sought after political gurus in the Midwest and president of the Paroska Group.

Years have gone by now and I've had a lot of thrilling moments.

In 1990, the United States Junior Chamber of Commerce named me the Best Young Mayor in America and honored me at their National Convention in Washington, D.C. Joe Farrell came with me on that trip, having been elevated to Council President. *The Euclid News Journal* sent a reporter to the nation's capital to cover the festivities.

As we sat up on the dais in the ballroom of a posh DC hotel, Nancy and I joined in with Joe and Ginny Farrell in marveling how things had changed from the bad old days of the Coalition.

With President Bush tied up in the War Room, Senator Bob Dole substituted and offered his congratulations for the Best Young Mayor Award. From left to right: Joe Farrell, Senator Dole, Ginny Farrell, Nancy, and me.

I had the pleasure of swearing-in the first minority to wear the uniform of the Euclid Police Department. Black employees found their way onto the city roster in every department. Jack Johnson became the first black municipal assistant finance director ever hired in Northeast Ohio and eventually he would become the City of Euclid's Director of Finance. Today, three members of city council are minorities.

No one would have imagined such events back in 1987. I like to think I had something to do with laying the foundation for Euclid's emergence into the light. The Police Minstrel shows of the 1950's seem like a memory from a previous age.

A collateral benefit of changing a ttitudes toward r ace was the enhancement of the city's relationship with its congressman, the

Honorable Louis Stokes, brother of former Cleveland Mayor Carl Stokes. Stokes was a founding member of the Congressional Black Caucus and Chairman of the powerful Ways and Means Committee. Stokes gained international prominence when he chaired a special select committee that reopened the investigation of the JFK assassination, ultimately refuting many of the conclusions of the Warren Commission.

Giunta and Rocco, however, never took advantage of the opportunities made possible through Stokes as an ally. Here was Stokes, one of the most influential persons in all of America, and Giunta just could not warm to the idea of having a black congressman. I changed all that.

Meeting Lou Stokes at his office.

Stokes was delighted to see a progressive thinker in the mayor's seat and he took me under his wing. Stokes raised a lot of eyebrows when he embraced this up-and-coming Republican. But he was a man of integrity. He often kidded me about my youth, noting that I had attended junior high with his brother's son, Carl Stokes Junior. Lynch and Stokes became a productive team for Euclid, the congressman getting me an audience one-on-one in the oval office with President Clinton.

Congressman Stokes really made me a hero when he granted my request to fund the Sims Park project. Sheer cliffs at the City's lakefront park made Lake Erie inaccessible for sunbathing and swimming. Stokes inserted millions of dollars in the Federal budget to create a beautiful beach to replace the cliffs. The Army Corps of Engineers oversaw this mammoth engineering feat.

I'll never forget the sight of scores of barges bringing in millions of tons of powdery sand, creating a sort of beach harbor. Sims Park to this very day remains one of the jewel recreation spots on America's North Coast, a fantastic dock having been added recently.

My relationship with Congressman Stokes showed doing the right thing bears fruit for the benefit of all. While we disagreed on some issues, I was proud to call the congressman my friend. Republican bigwigs ostracized me because I was rubbing elbows with one the nation's leading Democrats. I didn't care. Lou Stokes in Congress was like having Babe Ruth batting cleanup. He got things done.

And Lake Erie? I made sure that the City of Euclid came to her rescue. With City Council's help, the Lynch administration launched the largest single effort to eliminate cross connections between storm and sanitary sewer lines in the history of the state of Ohio.

The federal government helped us pay the almost one hundred million dollar tab, but it was worth it. Beaches and fishing areas are again fit for human enjoyment. King Neptune holds court in the splendor of water so clean you can drink it.

Perhaps the most surprising part of being elected Mayor of Euclid was the megaphone it gave me to affect change. Teddy Roosevelt used to call it the "bully pulpit". Essentially, I discovered that people paid attention to what I had to say.

It was quite a culture shock to be transformed from irrelevant to important in one night in November. On two occasions, my newly installed ability to get people's attention simply because I was the mayor made a big difference in the lives of people in need.

Vice-President Dan Quayle came to see me: Joe Farrell looks on.

Jesse Jackson, running for president, came to Euclid: He told us to keep hope alive.

Senator John McCain was stumping in Ohio in 2008.

The first was Doug Flood. I was watching the 11 o'clock news one night when the medical report featured a story about a man dying of an unusual form of cancer.

Doug Flood contracted a rare blood cancer that was threatening to take his life, absent meaningful medical intervention. Unfortunately, no effective treatment was available save an experimental drug called Fludarabine. Fludarabine, however, was unavailable to Mr. Flood because the National Institute of Health did not include him in their testing protocol. As an experimental drug, Fludarabine did not yet have FDA approval.

The TV reporter sadly concluded that Doug Flood was out of luck and because of the progress of the disease, out of time.

I found the whole thing disturbing. After all, if Doug Flood was dying and was left with no treatment options, what harm would occur if Flood was given access to the experimental Fludarabine.

I called the television station and obtained additional information, including Doug Flood's phone number. After interviewing Flood and his wife, I headed off to Washington where I just happened to have a meeting with federal officials at the Department of Housing and Urban Development.

After my scheduled meetings concluded, I made a beeline for the National Institute of Health. I introduced myself as the Mayor of Euclid and asked to see the doctor in charge of the Fludarabine experimental protocol.

The doctor took the time to explain the position of the federal government and was sincere in telling me his hands were tied. Doug Flood could not receive the drug because the federal rules required that recipients be part of a previously identified list of patients participating in an approved program. I told him how much I appreciated his dedication to the federal regulations and how I admired the nobility of the work he was doing.

However, I told him I was prepared to camp outside his office until Doug Flood received the potentially life-saving experimental drug. The doctor was flummoxed and I could tell he was calculating the impact of CNN running a story about the Mayor who wouldn't leave, risking arrest in a valiant effort to save the life of a stranger.

The doctor from the National Institute of Health made me wait for two hours.

Then he agreed to release the drug to Doug Flood. Amazingly, the unapproved medicine did the trick and Doug Flood is a healthy, happy dad and husband still kicking today.

Then there is the story of Kourtaney Collins, the little girl who made you fall in love the moment you met her. I caught wind of the plight of Kourtaney Collins from a friend of mine in the nearby community of Willoughby, Ohio.

Kourtaney, at the age of one and a half, had been the target of a developmental disease called Hurler's Syndrome that attacked all her vital organs and worse, would lead to her eventual death without a specialized form of bone marrow transplant. The only hospital capable of this sensitive pediatric bone marrow transplant was Iowa City Hospital in Iowa.

Lacking the necessary insurance, Kourtaney's family was chagrined to learn that the life-saving procedure would not go forward unless they coughed up prepayment of the $400,000 cost. Fundraising was underway by the Willoughby Frontier Days Committee, but little Kourtaney's health was failing rapidly. Things looked dim for the cute kid who had won my heart.

I contacted the Iowa City Hospital administrator. I personally pledged that the four hundred thousand dollar cost would be paid out of my own pocket if necessary. The news services all around the country picked up the story. The hospital, faced with this very public gesture by this now high-profile mayor, relented. Iowa City Hospital agreed to operate immediately.

Kourtaney is living a joyful life to this very day, having survived many years beyond the original life expectancy predicted by her doctors. We occasionally get together for some laughs with her mom and her grandfather, Dan Brindley, who has kept an especially close eye on Kourtaney over the years. Kourtaney's giggle is infectious.

Interestingly enough, the various fundraising activities for Kourtaney continued and it was more than enough to pay the Iowa City Hospital tab. My personal pledge ended up costing me not one dime. Lucky thing: my mayor salary would not have been near enough. But again, it's an example of how the mere position of mayor can be used to solve real human problems. God bless the voters and Kourtaney Collins.

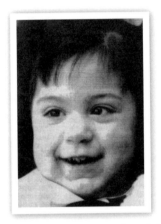

Kourtaney Collins needed a miracle and she got one.

I was elected to a second term despite an aggressive attempt at a comeback by my old nemesis, then former Mayor Tony Giunta. This time I had a more comfortable margin of victory as 79% of the voters cast their ballots in my favor, the highest margin of victory by a Euclid mayoral candidate facing an opponent in our city's history.

Mayor Giunta suffered a fatal heart attack almost exactly one year from the date of this lopsided defeat. Maybe it was just too much for him. I've heard it said by some that he died of a broken heart.

With the help of Congressman Stokes, President Clinton invited me to confer with him in the Oval Office in 1993. It was a productive meeting. Nancy came with me and as we joked around with the President of the United States, Nancy gave me a familiar look.

"Holy Crap!"

Heady stuff.

Left to right: Nancy's sister Patti, Nancy, the President, and me. Patti came along for the ride and was invited to join us at the White House at the last second.

But nothing will ever compare to that campaign of 1987 and the remarkable night that made all the work and self-doubt worth it all.

It's not likely that the Smithsonian will erect a display related to these amazing events.

But I was there.

And I assure you this incredible story is true.

Euclid was changed forever.

For the good.

It's a story of standing up to the forces of evil and living to tell the tale.

And there is a message for the David Lynch's of the future. Don't give up. Reach for the impossible goal. Win or lose, you are better off for trying.

And the impossible just might happen.

Joe Farrell died in 1997 from pancreatic cancer.

Here's to you, Joe. Couldn't have done it without you.

If you've a kitchen table in heaven, I'll be visiting you one late night in the future.

And we'll relive the whole damn thing all over again.

Beer's in the fridge.

Photo Credits
in Order of Appearance

Photo Credits

in Alphabetical Order According to Source